WHY ME?

AN AUTOBIOGRAPHY

by

Baron Daniels

Table of Contents

CHAPTER 1

I hope my story inspires each of you in all the days of your lives. To understand that God loves us all and wants the best for His children. With all my ups and downs, the things I've learned along the way have been amazing. More times than I can count, death has knocked at my door, but God didn't allow it. God must have a plan for me to achieve before He gives death permission. I must find out what that is. Why me, God? What is my purpose? What is Your will for my life? How do I begin? Where do I start? What must happen in my life to hear His voice before it's too late? To understand, journey back with me when I was a child. My first memory was sitting in the back seat of a car.

I must have been four or five years old, drinking a soda out of a bottle. Whoever was driving hit the brakes just as I went for another drink, and the tip of the bottle hit my front two upper teeth and knocked them completely out. I swallowed one, and the other went inside the bottle. This was the early 1970s, when you were taught as boys to stop crying, man up, and that they would grow back. "Go and lay down and take a nap." My mother would clean houses for a living or work at the local dry cleaner's. My dad? I didn't know him. I don't remember who was driving the car when my teeth were knocked out, but I know it was a man.

I remember very little about living in New Jersey. We moved to West Palm Beach, Florida, in the mid-1970s. My brother and I were left home alone a lot when Mom went to work. There was no daycare or babysitters back then. We got our instructions from her, and that's the way it went. Mom would say, "I'm going to work. Don't go outside. Don't open the door for anyone, or there will be some ass whipping when I get home. Don't let anybody tell me you were outside or saw anyone in this house. Your sandwiches are in the refrigerator for lunch. Do you understand me?" she said. Of course, we said, "Yes, ma'am." We did just that for a while. We would watch TV or look out the window at all the other kids running around playing while we were stuck in the house. We had to try to have fun inside. We watched the Superman TV show all the time—how he would jump out of the window and fly. One day I wanted to fly too, and our refrigerator handle had been broken for a while. The top of the handle was pointy and sharp.

On this day, I tied a long towel around my neck, put on some long socks for my super boots, and climbed on top of the fridge. I stood up and said, "Up, up, and away!" and jumped. My cape got caught under my feet, and I went straight down. My face hit the handle and split my upper lip into two. Like paper, it was completely split. My brother screamed. I screamed and cried. He took me to the old lady next door, and when she saw me, she screamed. We didn't have a telephone to call Mom, so we had to wait for her to get home. We went back to the house, and I laid down. Mom came in and screamed. She rushed me to the hospital. I had to be stitched up. I remember them putting me on the bed to start stitching. I jumped off the bed and took off down the hall, screaming and crying, looking for my mom. I saw her and got hold of her leg, holding on for dear life. The doctor sent two big, giant men to get me to bring me back. Mom was crying too, but she was helping them peel me off her leg. I could see her standing there as they took me back to the room.

Here I was, a five- or six-year-old kid, and Mom wasn't coming to help me. They held me down from head to toe. I mean, I was on lockdown. And they stitched me up good. After that, Mom got on the landlord's case and made him replace the refrigerator. My lips healed up pretty well, and best believe you me, I didn't do that again. Not long after, school started. Getting ready for the first day of kindergarten was scary—being left alone with all these strange people. We lived in a rooming house, and I didn't understand what that meant or why my mother was living in the building with strange people.

My name is Baron Teon Knight. I was very shy around lots of people I didn't know. My childhood wasn't the best. It was challenging, to say the least. As a child wanting to have fun and play, it wasn't a whole lot of that for me. By the time I was old enough to start school, it was like my mom was dropping me off on the first day and leaving me alone with all these big people and lots of kids. She made me get on the bus each day and go to school. I was afraid. The big people and kids seemed okay. We sat at tables in the room and played games. I didn't know these were learning games. I felt lost and ashamed because I wasn't learning as fast as the other kids. But I soon caught on how to put a puzzle together and started to solve it by myself. I soon fell back into the feeling of being ashamed. I wasn't as smart as the other kids in class.

By the time I reached the third grade, I was in a special education class. That meant I was slow and unable to read like the other kids. Reading was my kryptonite, and the other kids and teachers knew it. I struggled even with the smallest words. One-on-one with my teacher didn't help either. They would send me home with homework to study and prepare for the upcoming spelling test. With really no support at home, my mom didn't finish school herself. With an eighth-grade education, she wasn't much help. Man, did I struggle trying to learn to read and write. And when it came to bullying because I was a dark-skinned kid, the jokes about being blacker or darker than the other kids had a tremendous emotional effect on me.

Being called a dummy, blacky, tar baby, midnight, or black knight was torture. This was done regularly, and I remember not saying anything to my mom, being afraid of being called a punk or told to "stop crying like a little bitch." "Let the other kids say what they want to," she'd say. "Just as long as they don't put their hands on you." Those old clichés, "sticks and stones may break your bones, but words can never hurt," well, let me tell you, those words hurt the hell out of me.

I wasn't a fighter and got beat up a few times. Between third and sixth grade, life at school and home didn't get any better. Mom had a few boyfriends, and we moved every year. I never knew who or where my biological father was. All she said was that his name was Tony and he lived in Newark. Like I knew where that was. After school, I would come home and the lights would be off, or the water would be off. Many times, the lights and water would be off at the same time. My brother and I never learned to call our mom "Mom." We grew up calling her Ja, short for Jerry. She never enforced it. I guess she accepted it. I would ask Mom, "Why don't we have any lights?" Back in those days, asking your parents questions like that was disrespectful, and you were punished.

Black kids knew their place when it came to our parents. We would have to get out the candles right before sunset and put a couple in each room for light. I would force myself to fall asleep so I didn't have to sit in the dark. There would be many nights like that, and it was extremely hard to do. When the water was off, I had to go outside to urinate behind the apartment or next door to a neighbor's. If I had to have a bowel movement, I used the toilet that already had feces in it from three other people. My brother and I had to take a bucket and ask the neighbor if we could fill it with water so we could flush our toilet. At first, I was ashamed, but that became the norm. I couldn't understand why this was always happening to us. When I looked out the window or out the door, all the other houses had lights. That made some of the neighborhood kids pick on and laugh at my brother and me. Even in school, they would tell other kids I had no lights, that I sat in the dark every night, or they'd tell them about the water being off too. What could I say or do? No one knew how hurt I was inside from all the teasing and the mean things that were said to me. Damn! I hated the nighttime because our power was off all the time. My mom's boyfriend at the time showed me how to turn the power back on.

Here I was, an eight-year-old kid in the back of the house, messing with the electric meter that must have had thousands of volts running through it, turning the lights back on. When the light company came out and disconnected the power because the bill wasn't paid, I would reconnect the power before nightfall. Once the power company realized we kept reconnecting the power, they took the meter. That didn't stop me from getting the power back. Because of my hatred for the night, I would scope out an empty house and steal the meter. I learned how to wait until nightfall to hook it up and remove it by 8:00 a.m. Monday through Friday. This went on for a while until the power company disconnected the power from the top of the pole.

At this point, we had to think outside the box about what to do to get power so we could watch TV like the neighbors. Mom's boyfriend decided to take the car battery out of the car and cut the power cord of the TV to expose the wires. He ran one wire to the positive side and the other to the negative, and we had power to the TV. That got us by for a few days until Mom was able to have the power legally turned back on. Monday morning, time for school, I was pretty much on my own—a third grader getting up, dressed, and walking to the bus stop by myself. By that time, I attended Kirklane Elementary. I was still afraid, but I pushed myself to go, have fun, and eat breakfast and lunch. I was sure at some point the power or water would go off again. I really think this hindered my learning in school.

I learned other things about life at a very young age. Sitting in the front of the bus, watching the bus driver shifting gears — his hands and feet coordination was smooth as ice. I didn't know I was learning something just by watching because this wasn't a classroom setting. Lord knows I tried to keep up with the other kids but couldn't. I felt stupid because the Black kids would start picking on me. I felt bad. I made the decision to hide in the restroom or go to the park all day. I would leave the house for school but rarely went to class. Instead, I got off the bus and went directly to the restrooms all day just to avoid being picked on.

Sometime during the early part of the school year, we moved to a different apartment across town, and I had to switch schools. Now I was attending Palm View Elementary. I was so happy I could make new friends, and no one would pick on me. At home, we'd have power and water like the other kids in the neighborhood — or so I thought. At first, it seemed my brother and I had everything we needed. Mom registered me in school, and I was off on my own.

CHAPTER 2

I remember sitting in the third grade on the first day, and it started again. The name-calling and teasing from the new kids: "Hey, Blackie!" or "Darkie!" "Blackie? Why are you calling me that?" I would ask. "My name is Baron Knight!" "Knight?" they'd say. "Yeah, you're right—you are Black, just like the night." I was crushed emotionally.

Here I was in a new place, and it was the same treatment. I absolutely hated my skin being so dark and was afraid to physically fight back. Just like at the old school, I had to take it and ask myself, "Why me?" I continued struggling in class. Just putting two words together was difficult for me. I thought I was ugly—Black as tar—and my last name being Knight only added fuel to the fire. Once again, I found myself hiding in the restrooms throughout the week. The only teacher who missed me in class and really cared about all her students was Ms. Carl. She started asking questions: "Why are you missing so much school?" She sent me home with a piece of paper for my mom. Because I couldn't read, I didn't know the paper had the same questions on it that Ms. Carl had asked me. My mom asked, "What's going on? You leave the house every morning, but you're not in school." Back in the day, parents ruled. No nonsense, all about respect, and every answer was "Yes, ma'am," "No, ma'am," "Yes, sir," or "No, sir."

I had to tell the truth because the beating was coming anyway, and she came with the thunder. "The kids are picking on me by calling me names because I'm Black," I said. She initially thought I meant the white kids. "Boy, don't let those white kids do that," she said. "No, ma'am, it's the Black kids who don't like me and are calling me stupid." "Boy, go outside and get me a switch off the tree so I can beat your ass. And you better not come back here with a small one, or I'll beat you with the whole tree!"

That was a long and slow walk, looking for that switch. All the trees had big and long branches. I remember breaking one off, walking back to the house, and plucking the leaves off. Another long walk, crying and talking to myself, hoping the switch wasn't too small because I didn't want to get beat with the whole tree. Mom said, "Take your pants off." She wanted the switch to hit all skin. And in a strange kind of way, I was glad she was beating the Black skin I hated—the skin that caused most of my problems in school. That midnight skin had kids saying, "We can't see you unless you smile and show your teeth so we can see your face," while they laughed. When the beating started, it was painful and long-lasting. Nothing like getting a beating and being yelled at all at the same time. But I thought, "Hit me harder—I hate my skin anyway." Growing up, I fell in love with the TV show Batman. I knew when it was on and made sure I was in place to watch. Bruce and Dick would run to the Bat-poles in regular clothes, slide down, and within seconds, they'd be Batman and Robin. They'd run to the Batmobile and peel out to the commissioner's office to fight crime. I didn't care about the other superheroes—Batman was the one. And to this very day, at fifty-four years old, he still is.

Along with the beatings came no TV. Mom knew taking the TV away was worse than the beatings. Beat me ten times over, but don't take Batman away. That made me go to all my classes and take whatever was coming my way—and it did. The struggle was real. Between the third and sixth grade, we moved so much that I went to five different elementary schools.

On the weekends, my friends and I would walk around different areas of West Palm Beach looking for something to do. We made our way downtown, walking in and out of businesses. We went into a Woolworth store, and while looking around, we noticed they had a restaurant in the back. We saw people sitting down, eating, and then going to the front of the store to pay for their meals afterward. So, we wondered if we could get away with eating and not paying. You would have thought they'd question two little kids to see if we had any money, but they didn't. We sat down, just the two of us, and like clockwork, the waitress came over. We ordered hamburgers and French fries. The food came, and we ate like kings—two big sandwiches, fries, and soda. We got up nervously but calm and smooth, like butter, and walked out the front door.

Once we made it outside, we took off running and laughing, giving each other high fives. How easy was that? We knew it was wrong, but we did it anyway. Because we were already downtown, we wondered what else we could get into. We walked up to people asking for money. There were payphones all over the place, and we would check every change slot for coins. As some weeks passed, we wanted to order more food again. Surely, they wouldn't remember us. We went back, sat down, and ordered the same thing! That juicy burger came out, and we ate like kings again.

We got up, walked right out the front door again, and ran. That was crazy. They must have been stupid! It made us want to do more and more. But our luck was about to change. Since we couldn't go downtown for a while, we decided to steal oranges from a tree in someone's backyard that was fenced in. It was a cement wall we had to climb over to get to them. For this heist, we had to get creative. We cupped our shirts like kangaroo pouches to carry out all the stolen fruit over the wall. Once over, we took off running to a safe place to sit down and eat. Damn, that was too easy! The very next day, we went back for more oranges. We jumped over the wall, got to the tree, and started plucking. The next thing I felt was pain coming from my back and the top of my head. I heard my friend screaming and crying.

Once I realized what was happening, the owner was beating us with a stick. I mean, you would have thought this old lady knew kung fu. She was beating our asses GOOD! We dropped all the oranges, running to the wall to get away. She must have run track in her heyday because she was right behind us, still swinging and connecting, lol. She beat us all the way up the wall, yelling at us. I don't know about my friend, but when I got home, my mom asked, "What happened to your head and arms?" I was too scared to lie to her. I told her what happened. I got another beating from her, and I had to go back to the house I stole from, knock on the door, and apologize to the old lady.

I remember her saying, "Baby, all you had to do was ask for some oranges. I would have given you plenty." She made me go back, pick up all the fruit that fell to the ground, and rake up all the leaves. I bagged it all and put it on the trash pile on the street. From that point, I was allowed to go over any time because I became somewhat of a cleanup boy. "If you want something, you need to work for it," Mom and the old lady said. "That little boy you're hanging out with is a troublemaker. I don't want to see you with him anymore," they said. But I didn't listen. He didn't come back to my house, but we would meet downtown. "Let's go get us a burger." Let me tell you, the gig was up. We walked in, sat down, and immediately they recognized us. "Get up and get out," they said. "You two didn't pay the last time you were here." The man grabbed us both by the arm, threw us out, and said, "Don't ever come back. If I see your faces again, I'm calling the police." We never went into that store again. However, we continued to hang out downtown. In one area, there was a wishing well—or at least that's what we called it—where people would throw pennies, nickels, dimes, and quarters. All we saw was free money. Of course, we started casing it out and planning how to get it. We waited until late in the evening to dive in as fast as possible and grab the shiny ones. "No pennies," we said. We went back every chance we had, especially on the weekends.

Once we had enough money to buy something to eat, we did. There were a couple of bus stations downtown—Greyhound and

Trailways. Both had small chairs with TVs that had quarter slots. If you put the money in, you could watch TV for fifteen minutes per quarter. They also had food vending machines with sandwiches and small snacks. The stolen money from the well-funded all of this. One day, we had no money and decided to go to the Trailways station to force open the vending machine to get some food. One of us was the lookout, and the other was the muscle.

I tried to open the slot with the sandwiches. It wouldn't budge at all. I got to the slot with some yogurt. Here's the thing: as you buy something from a slot, the machine rotates and refills it with the same item. The yogurt slot opened for me. I must have had eight or nine yogurts in hand. The lookout kid didn't look out very well because the lady saw me. She knew what we were doing, came from behind the counter, and popped both of us several times. Then, she made us eat every stolen yogurt we had. I was sick to my stomach. To this very day, I still can't eat yogurt. We didn't have anything else to do but walk around, trying not to get into more trouble. Still, we found ourselves doing silly things like throwing rocks at passing trains or putting our hands inside vending machines to try to reach the candy or chips in the bottom row.

We were just two kids with very little food at home. There was no breakfast, lunch, or dinner in my house — just a bowl of cornflakes for dinner. There were a couple of local pool halls with pinball machines. The owner knew I didn't have any money to play the pinball machines, so he would let me come in on Saturday mornings and vacuum the floors and sweep the pool tables. I had to put all the cue sticks in the racks nice and neat, take out the trash, and clean the windows. He would give me five to six dollars. I didn't tell anyone I had money. I would play a few games, then go to the store and buy something to eat at midday. Don't get me wrong, we had food, but it had to last us all week. Nothing like today, where kids can eat all day at will. We had to ask for permission before we could eat or drink anything besides water.

With all that going on at this time in my life, from time to time, we had to live with different people, sleeping on the floor because we would get evicted. How inconvenient that must have been for the people we were living with, taking in a woman and her two kids. I don't remember the length of time we lived with different people, but it happened quite often. Mom decided to move to Pahokee, Florida, and we lived with my uncle. The bad thing about that was he lived in a rooming house with his girlfriend and their little girl. Damn! All of us were in one room—six people. It was bad. My uncle and his girlfriend had the bed, the little girl had the small couch, and we slept on the hard floor. My uncle was barely making it himself, and now here we come. At some point, we moved into a rooming house down the street. Three was better than six, but we slept in one room and shared the kitchen and bathroom with the other ten tenants.

We had to keep a Styrofoam cooler with ice in the room for our food. Sandwich meat and a gallon of fruit punch, milk, and in those days, if you wanted water, you just went to the water faucet in the kitchen with an old mayonnaise jar and filled it up to drink. Or, if you were outside playing, we would drink water from the water hose. If you left your food in the kitchen of a rooming house, someone would eat your food or drink whatever juice you had. We tried labeling our food and leaving it in the refrigerator, but it didn't work. And when you asked who ate your food, everyone played dumb and stupid. The safest thing to do for food was to keep a cooler in your room. You had to bring your own toilet paper with you and keep that in your room as well. We had to wear sandals to take a shower; the building shower was nasty — the bathroom, period, was nasty. The building was rat-infested; you could hear them inside the walls. It was a mess living like that. There wasn't much to do living in Pahokee, but I think I tried to make the best of it.

A game room uptown was where most of the kids would go to hang out. Whatever the latest video games were at the time, or you played pool. The owner or one of his kids would be there all the time, walking around with an apron on, exchanging dollars for quarters so the customers could play games. I had no money to play. Most of the time, I stood around watching the other kids having fun. If I didn't go uptown, I would hang around in the front yard or play inside the building. My uncle would come by sometimes and take me fishing. I wasn't very good at it; I was too scared of the worms and terrified of the fish when he caught one. I got enrolled in Pahokee Elementary, but that didn't last very long. I wasn't engaged at all, mainly there for lunch and P.E.

One night, my brother and I were home alone, and it was raining and lightning. We didn't have cable but had a small TV with a pair of rabbit ear antennas. Batman was coming on, and the channel wouldn't come in clear, no matter how much I adjusted the antenna. All I got was snow and static on the screen. Batman was fading in and out. I'd only heard about God a few times at this point in my life. None of the family went to church or ever had a Bible. They did go to the bars and local clubs, but church — not a one of us. The little I knew about God came from Christmas-time TV shows. Batman wasn't coming in clear enough to see, and I started cursing this so-called God out. Out of my mouth, I was using the bad words I had heard from the streets and home. "F God, I hate God, God can kiss my A — ." I mean, I went on a rampage. The next thing I knew, I had just moved away from the TV, and a big bolt of lightning came through the window and hit the TV. A big boom! And a flash came through the window. No damage to the glass window, but it destroyed the TV. No fire, just a big puff of smoke. That's when I knew whoever this God was; he was real, he heard me, and he spared me. I know now, by his mercy and grace, he decided to hit the TV instead of me. My brother and I were scared to move, so we went to sleep. Seemed like Batman almost got me killed.

Here I was in a little old country town and another elementary school, and the pressure was on. Pahokee Elementary wasn't too bad. Most of the kids were nice to me, I think because they had very little. We lived in Pahokee for about six months, and Mom decided to move back to West Palm Beach. At this point, I think she was approved to be on Section 8 housing, and we got a nice brand-new apartment in Riviera Beach on 8th Street. It felt like rags to riches, she came into some money or something. I don't know what she did to get what we got. My brother and I finally had our own rooms, and I was going to the 6th grade with a brand-new attitude. Initially, it started off very well, a new school, a new apartment, new furniture, food in the refrigerator, water and power, it seemed everything was perfect. Suddenly, in my brother's room, Mom allowed him to put playboy centerfolds as wallpaper in his room. The wall was covered with naked women all over the place, and I saw it all, legs opened, breast hanging, and asses out. I wasn't allowed to, but he could. By that time, he had dropped out of middle school. And when his birthday came, she would get all her friends and his friends together and throw a big house party. Lots of food and alcohol, music would be jumping, people would be dancing and walking all through the apartment, and mom would be hosting, playing cards, and smoking cigarettes.

I tried to fit in as much as possible, but it was all his and her friends. Something in my head, like a small voice, started to make me wonder and think. Why didn't I have birthday parties? I have a birthday too. And when I asked, she would say you're too little to have parties. I didn't get anything really at all for my birthdays, nothing that I can remember. Thinking back, my brother had parties all the time. I just had to accept what she said, or there would be consequences. My brother is her favorite. He had already had a baby, and girls would be over all the time. Because we were on section eight, and mom only had to pay three dollars a month in rent. The landlord would come early Saturday morning to collect his three dollars. Mom would get very upset and be cursing at herself because of the time he came. She would always sleep in the living room on the couch. Her room had a hole bedroom set in it, but she didn't sleep in there.

On Saturday mornings, because of my love for morning cartoons and Batman, I had to be very quiet and watch TV with the volume very low not to wake her up. Sitting on the floor as close as I could be to the tv. For some reason, when we had power, the TV stayed on all night, even when she was asleep. And if I came out of my room quietly and turned the channel because she was sleeping, and if she woke up and saw me watching something different, she would be upset. She would say, "Boy, who told you to turn that channel?" School was coming and heading to the 6th grade, but still on the 5th-grade level. I still couldn't read that well and was not too good at math. I started looking at pictures with words on them to figure out what the word says. Forcing myself to get better and better. I didn't know how far I would make it at West Riviera Elementary before we moved again. By the time I made it to sixth grade, I went to Kirk Lane Elementary, Palm View Elementary, Perrine Elementary, Palm Springs Elementary, Pahokee Elementary, and West Riviera, just to give you an idea of how much we moved. The teachers weren't very helpful here at West Riviera.

I remember raising my hand to ask her a question. She called me up at her desk. I walked up with my book in hand I needed her to help me read. She said Knight, do you see all these kids in here? Yes, ma'am, she said go back to your desk and ask one of them to help you. And she went back to picking her nails, looking at me like I was not worth her time or day. That was not happening. Why would I do that? I'm not asking the kids anything, I said to myself. To give them a reason to start doing what the other kids have done, picking and teasing me. I struggled through the whole year just to stay above average. My report card reflected C's and D's only to wind up going to summer school to barely pass to the seventh grade. Between the sixth and seventh grade is when I met a kid named Octavius, who would become my best friend and home boy for life. Tavis and I would become inseparable.

I was one year older than Tavis. It was Christmas time, and he was outside riding his bike. I made a few other friends, too, and they were all out riding. I didn't get or have a bike, and when I asked some of the other kids if I could ride their bikes, they said no. They said their mom said not to let anyone ride their bikes. But I asked Tavis, and he let me ride and have fun, too. He saw me just standing there watching all the other boys having fun riding up and down the street. We started hanging out every day, meeting each other's families. One day, Tavis came over and said his house did not have power. No power, I said. I know how that feels. We sometimes don't have power, either. Tavis and I came to realize we had a common problem; it blew our minds. That our home and upbringing would be one and the same. Depending on what utility was off, the other one had. If my water was off, I could go to his to use the bathroom or take a bath. If Tavis had no power, he could come to my house and watch TV. We had to piece together food when food was scarce. There were days when one of us would have peanut butter and jelly but no bread. I would say, "Bring that over here because we have bread," and we would make sandwiches and fill our bellies. If either one of us had no food and had to wait for our moms to come later in the evening, we would walk the neighborhood looking for empty Coca-Cola bottles.

In the mid-1980s, the local convenience stores would give you ten cents per bottle because the soda companies would reuse the bottles. We would find as many as we could and buy something to eat. We would buy Twinkies, potato chips, and Yoo-hoos. And if we couldn't find any bottles, we would find a mango tree, climb it, and sit in the tree eating mangos. We both had older siblings and single moms. Both of our moms seemed to always move every year, and whoever moved, he and I would still find a way to hang out together, even if it meant walking to meet halfway and walking back together to each other's house, then doing the reverse. He and I had conversations trying to understand why we were always struggling with not having water, electricity, food, and moving all the time. There was no father figure in our houses. Both of our moms had boyfriends in and out, but most of the time, they were single. Tavis's and my uncles were more involved and were the only father figures we had. Tavis was the first person who didn't pick on me because I was dark-skinned. He was high yellow, what we now call redbone. He was smart and was an A and B student. He didn't laugh at me because I didn't read well. He helped me study with my homework all the time. If I had to guess, he wanted me to pass my classes more than I did. Every Sunday afternoon, an old TV show called Kung Fu Theater would come on. It played kung fu movies all day. Of course, Bruce Lee was everyone's favorite.

We used to practice with each other all the time. There were no kung fu schools around, so we decided to take karate at the local gym. It was 20 dollars a month, and the karate uniforms were 50 dollars. I don't remember how we got the money to join the class, but we did. I think we went to class three times a week. After a few weeks of training and watching Bruce Lee movies, Tavis and I used to walk around the neighborhood in our karate uniforms like we were the baddest mofos around. We would walk up and down the street wishing someone would pick a fight with us so we could kick some ass. Tavis used to say, "We'll kick ass and take names later." He had a pair of homemade nunchucks inside his pants, lol. You would have thought we were in Hong Kong. He and I practiced with each other all the time. His sister Victoria, who is now my sister, laughed at us all the time, watching her little brothers in the living room or outside in the front yard training. The karate teacher signed us up for a karate tournament in Orlando. Tavis and I were white belts, and at home, we practiced what moves we were going to use on our opponents.

We got to Orlando ready to rumble, ready to get our Bruce Lee on, only to find out we had to fight each other. This was a problem. I didn't want to fight my best friend. But they gave us no choice. Here we were in this big stadium with hundreds of people watching. We got into the middle of the mat; the ref gave us our instructions. I said to myself, "I'm going to throw light jabs, a couple of small body shots, nothing to hurt him. I mean, this is my homeboy, my brother, my best friend." After a few minutes, this fool (Tavis) must have forgotten who the big brother was. I'm 10 pounds heavier and a few inches taller. He hit me in the mouth with everything he had, busting my bottom lip and making me bleed—with a smile on his face. Suddenly, that homeboy shit went out the window. I remember how Bruce Lee acted when someone hit him in the face. He would taste the blood, wipe his face, see the blood on his hand, look at the one that hit him, and holler. I did just that. I went in on Tavis like Bruce Lee, Chuck Norris, and John Wick all in one. The ref had to pull me off his ass, lol. I won the first-place trophy. We laughed all the way home. "Man, look at my lip," I said to him. "My shit is swollen." That was the last time he and I went to class. We would hang around the house after that. The landlord owned about 20 apartments in the area. Tavis and I wanted to make some money for snacks or for whatever we wanted. The landlord told us if we helped him clean and paint the empty apartments, he would pay us. Boy, did we jump on that offer. He had us wiping the walls, painting the walls, cleaning windows — the whole damn thing — getting them ready for the next tenants. I know we cleaned more than one apartment, and when it was time to pay up for all the work he and I did, the landlord gave us each 5 dollars.

We went home to show our moms how much we had made, and let me tell you, both moms (Jerry and Barbara) went off on him. They let him have it. They cursed him up the right side and down the left. "You should be ashamed of yourself, you cheap ass so-and-so, paying our kids 5 dollars for all that work they did. You better put your damn hands back into your pockets and bring some more money out, or there's going to be a problem." Tavis and I had no idea he had cheated us out of money. We were happy to have 5 dollars. After all the yelling they did, he had no choice but to pay us accordingly. I mean, we were only eleven and twelve years old. Tavis and I were such good friends, we didn't even have to ask to spend the night at each other's houses, especially on the weekends or in the summertime. We would stay up late waiting for our moms to fall asleep. Once they did, we would take the keys to the car, sneak outside, and put the car in neutral. We'd push the car away from the apartment so they couldn't hear us start it. We would drive all through the neighborhood at 2 a.m. We would take turns driving and then come back around 4 a.m. We had to get the car up to speed, turn it off with it in neutral, and coast up to the apartment to park it like it never moved. They had no idea we were having fun at night like that. Vicky didn't either because she slept hard as a rock. You had to call her three or four times if she was asleep before she even cracked her eyelids. We never got caught. We had fun. We would stay up almost all night just talking or cracking jokes on each other. Tavis and I would walk over to the drive-in theater and watch whatever movie was playing outside the gate. Some weekends, our moms would invite their friends over to our houses and play cards for money. They would never sit down at the table to play but would serve food and drinks from the bar we had. As time went on, I came to understand the host never played — they got paid for hosting and keeping order. When the gambling got heated and people started arguing, I had to stay outside or in my room. Mom would also go to the dog track and bet on dog races or to the bingo hall to gamble to make extra money.

When I wasn't hanging out with Tavis, I helped clean condos. My mom would sometimes take my brother and me to work with her. Going up to the penthouses at the top of the high-rise was amazing. She must have had fifteen clients in that building. Mom would even clean their condos when the owners were living up north. I watched her get down on her knees and scrub floors with her hands, wash their linens, wash dishes, and clean walls — basically from front to back, top to bottom. Summer came to an end, and I started middle school. The bus stop was fifty yards away; I could see it from my bedroom window. Like always, I would get myself up and dressed and be at the bus stop ahead of schedule. Back in those days, we had to report to homeroom every morning after breakfast and then go to class.

I was keeping up in my classes and comprehending some of the lessons, but I struggled to learn how to read, which made it very difficult for me to retain anything. I tried to study at home to prepare for a test. I think the best part of the 7th grade was breakfast, lunch, and going to P.E. so we could go outside and play. And again, it would really be difficult when I got home — there was no power and no water. But I was able to pass some of my classes throughout the year, though not enough to pass to the 8th grade. At the end of the year, I was assigned to go to summer school and still could not succeed. I ended up being held back. I had to repeat the 7th grade. I was really bummed out for the rest of the summer. What are the kids going to say? Are they going to laugh at me and call me stupid? I guess I'll find out.

CHAPTER 3

School started. I remember getting off the bus with my head down, ashamed that all my friends were in the 8th grade, and I was repeating the 7th grade. Come to find out, I had some 8th and 7th-grade classes. I had a few kids laugh at me but was able to keep going. As school continued, one of my classmates, I would notice walking down the street every day halfway through school. I was in P.E. outside playing and would see her. On the way to school the next day, I asked her, "When I see you walking, leaving school, where are you going?" She said, "I'm going to work." "Where do you work?" I asked. She said, "I work at Wendy's." She explained, "I come to school for my three major classes, which were math, English, and social studies. After that, I walk up to Wendy's and work three hours a day." That really got my attention, and I wanted to do that. She said, "It's part of the work program the school has. You have to be fourteen and pass your major classes. You are only allowed to work three hours a day, twenty-one hours a week." So, I went to the school guidance counselor to sign up for the program. I was so excited and ready to get my work on. I remember getting my very first interview, sitting in the lobby at Wendy's filling out the application. I was going to make three dollars and thirty-five cents an hour. I had no idea what that meant; all I knew was that I was ready.

I went through the process and got approved and hired within a month. I got my uniform and start date. I caught on fast, learning how to make sandwiches and working the grill and the French fry station. I worked for two weeks, and finally, I got paid a whole eighty-five dollars. In the early '80s, I was thirteen or fourteen, and I was rich. I had hit the jackpot; I mean, I had eighty-five dollars. I went home and showed Mom, not expecting her to say, "Hand it over. From now on, you will bring me the check, and I'll give you what I want you to have." She said, "Mama will put the rest of your money in the bank and save it for you." Initially, I was okay with that. I think she gave me fifteen dollars out of eighty-five dollars. This went on for some time — bringing her the check — and from time to time, things were still getting turned off. As school and work went on, I would ask her if I could have ten dollars of the money in the bank. She would say, "Mama had to use some of your money to get groceries." Or something to the effect of, "Mama had to use the money to pay a bill," but it made no sense. What bill could have been paid if the power or the water were still getting turned off? I was confused and inside mad — and I say inside because in the '80s, you were not allowed to ask too many questions. I had to go with the flow and continued bringing her the check. I started wanting my money for myself. It seemed like my brother was on easy street, and I was working for nothing. I finally got the nerve to start cashing my own check before I got home.

Little by little, I gave her what I wanted her to have. She pushed back, but I stood my ground respectfully. By then, I knew she wasn't saving anything for me. I wanted to buy my own clothes, candy, or ice cream when the ice cream truck came through. Or go to the local game room to play games and have fun. I couldn't do any of that. Just about every time I would ask, she didn't have it. Those were the days before home video games. We had no transportation at the time, but the school bus got me close enough where I walked to Wendy's. Getting home was a problem. I either had to walk three or four miles or catch a ride with my coworker. Mom did not make any kind of effort to make sure I could get home; I was on my own. I became skilled at Wendy's in all the positions, but trouble was right around the corner. Mom would get so upset when the landlord would come to collect his three dollars in rent early on Saturday mornings. "You don't have to come to my damn apartment so early in the morning, waking me up for three dollars." She decided to move again, to the next city, seven miles south. That meant now I'm almost eleven miles away from school and work.

Without a concern for me or without hesitation, we moved to a not-so-pleasant apartment. It was a dump; I mean, the bathroom didn't even have a floor. We had to walk on the floor studs to use the toilet and tub. We went from a nice brand new 3-bedroom to a crappy place. At the time, I didn't know what she was thinking. Because I was a cashier, I started to understand how money works. Making things make sense, three dollars wasn't anything to pay. All she had to do was give the man thirty-six dollars for the year and be done. Giving up section 8 was a terrible decision, but I had to think of something because I didn't want to switch schools again, and my job was right down the street from school. I was in a position no 7th grader should be in. In my own kind of way, I stood my ground and decided to stay at Walkins Jr High. I had to figure out how I was going to get from West Palm Beach to North Palm Beach. Well, this was a challenge I thought, and somehow, I knew if I could get to my old address, I could walk over to the school bus stop and catch the bus to school.

So, I had to get up two hours earlier and catch a cab, walk, or Mom would sometimes let me drive her car to the old address, park the car on the side of the road, and take the bus. I guess she felt bad, or she wanted that check to keep coming. And after school and work, I did the opposite to get home. There were some long days when I had to walk. I had my coworker's parents drop me off halfway sometimes. The struggle was real to be living where you don't want to be, and all my friends were miles away, and Mom and my brother seemed not to care.

In a few weeks, I started noticing I was having trouble catching my breath after I sneezed or coughed. It felt like my lungs were collapsing; it took all I had to suck in air to breathe. Something in that apartment was making me sick, but again, I had to man up and get over it when I had attacks. I made it to the end of the school year. I passed to the 8th grade, but 4 weeks before school was over, Mom decided we were going to move to San Antonio, TX. Dammit to myself! Texas? She wanted to move there because her baby brother lived there, and he could help her get on her feet. Because she worked for rich people who trusted her with their condos, she had keys to all of them. The rich people only lived there for part of the year; they would come down from up north in the winter months. Mom would clean the condominiums before they arrived and continued to do so with them there. A few weeks before the big move, she was coming home with all kinds of electronics and clothing. I am talking about small TVs, VCRs, cameras, and jewelry.

I wondered where all this stuff was coming from. Come to find out, she had stolen all those things from the condominiums that she cleaned.

Again, most of the owners were up north when she took that stuff — right past the door attendant and all. I cannot imagine what they thought when they came home and saw their property was missing. You know, VCRs in the 80s were the thing to have. Suddenly, she was having yard sales — little mini swap shops in front of the apartment. She even sold most of the furniture we had. My brother and I packed up what was left to take to Texas. We had maybe thirty boxes or so, all of which had to go to the bottom of a bus. We were moving to Texas via Greyhound bus. I remember the bag handler at the station said, "Ma'am, this is going to cost a lot of money to ship all these boxes." Between her getting all emotional, crying tears, and having a fit, the Greyhound employee did not charge her for all those boxes; he only charged her for half. I was sad too; I wasn't going to see my best friend again, leaving all my friends and my job. On the bus, riding off from town to town, it took us 2 days with all the stops to get to San Antonio.

My uncle picked us up. He had to make a few trips to the station to get all our boxes. Now, we were living with him and his new wife and baby. Déjà vu — the 3 of us were in 1 room again, and all the boxes were in his garage. It seemed okay for a minute, but then the tension was in the air. Having us there was an inconvenience — more food, more water, and more power being used. Mom finally found a place in town, something like a townhouse apartment. My uncle was moving fast to get us out. I mean, he was putting boxes all on top of his car. There was no talking, just moving, and when the last box was unloaded into the apartment, he got in the car and rode off into the sunset. There was no furniture, no TV, no transportation, and no food. A little corner store, one hundred yards away, is how we ate — peanut butter sandwiches and canned goods for a few days. My mom and brother found a job at a local cleaner's. I had to stay home all day long with nothing else to do. I started unpacking and putting labeled boxes away.

We had no TV or house phone; it was just the four walls. To take a break from unpacking, I walked around the apartment complex to learn my way around the area. I sat by the pool area for a while and walked up and down the street. Once back at the apartment, I unpacked more. In one of the boxes, I found a birth certificate. It read, "Baron Teon Daniels." Who is that? I asked myself. I was so confused and surprised at the same time. When Mom came home, I went right to her and showed her what I had found and asked who Baron Teon Daniels was. With hesitation, she said that it is your real name. She did not get into the reasons why she had me believe my name was Knight. She knew all this time and had my birth certificate hidden away in her closet somewhere, I guess. What and why would she do something like that? That made me feel unwanted at times; I just don't know why. I don't think my brother even knew either. In a way, I was glad too—I did not have to associate my last name with the darkness of my skin tone. The new kids would never know my old identity. I am now Baron Daniels! It came to me so easily, too. I was glad to get rid of Knight. I felt like a superhero who just discovered he or she had superpowers. It wasn't long before school started. I had to ask the local kids where and when the high school was and the bus stop. I registered myself, Baron Daniels. Just like I've done before, I got on the school bus and rode off to the unknown.

I didn't know where the school was, but I went because I wanted to finish. I got off the bus and went to the office with only my birth certificate. I registered myself into the ninth grade at MacArthur High. They asked a lot of questions that I couldn't answer, but they took me in and gave me a class schedule, and school began. Getting my class schedule, learning my way around campus, and making new friends. But something was different about this school—I started to notice it was dominantly white. I may have been the only Black kid in most of my classes. I did not feel like it because I was treated like one of them. I was addressed by my name, not by all the names my own people were calling me to hurt me. All my new friends in San Antonio were white. I was on the right track. While having fun outside in my physical education class, one of my teachers saw me running around with the other kids. He said, "Son, you run pretty fast. Have you ever played football?" I said, "Only in the streets or at the park with my friends back home." "Your speed would be something the football coach would like to see." He set me up to meet him and showcase my speed. The football coach said, "I hear that you are fast! Show me what you got." He brought over his fastest freshman football player and lined us up on the track. This kid was a little arrogant; he came over like Dutch from The Karate Kid, with a look on his face. He and I made eye contact on the line, the coach was down the track with the whistle. Head-to-head, that whistle blew, and we took off in a 40-yard dash. I didn't even see him running beside me at all. He got his butt spanked that day; some humble pie was handed out. The coaches were impressed, and they put me on the team. I was a running back. The coaches were hard on us — when one got in trouble, we all were in trouble. It made us bond together and practice harder. My problem was I could not remember the plays, but one: straight up the middle, and if I made it through, no one could catch me. Man, I practiced that play for weeks up until game day. I was physically ready and mentally nervous because this was my first high school game. I was also excited thinking that my mom would come to the game, but little did I know, she had no interest. It was on a Saturday; there was no reason she or my brother could not have come. My first game was a home game, and I was ready to rumble. The first play was called, and I missed a block, and my quarterback got sacked. The coach called me out for missing a block but called on me for the next play. When I got the ball, I ran up the middle, full speed, full power, and the kid tried to tackle me, hit me, grabbing me. I did a full spin and slung his ass off me around the 50-yard line. He must have gone 5 or 6 feet away. All I saw was an open field after that. The jets kicked in—Touchdown!! All my teammates came running down, high-fiving, pats on the ass, and head-butting helmets, cheering. That was the most exciting time I have ever had. What a rush of enjoyment. But with all of that, we lost the game, and I took some of the blame on myself because I knew only that one play. Once they figured that out, they had our number. I do not remember my jersey number, but I remember the coaches and the defense yelling, "Watch number 10 up the middle" —if that was my number, LOL. I cried on the bus coming home, and when I walked in the house, Mom was sitting on the couch smoking a cigarette. I do not recall her asking me anything about the game. Life went on in San Antonio for a while, then I started to miss home. All my friends, especially Tavis. I went outside into the apartment complex crying, and Mom came out and, for the first time, was consoling. I started to hang out around the area and saw a brand-new Wendy's under construction. I jumped right on it and filled out the application. Once it opened, I was hired right away. They did not have to train me at all; I just picked up where I left off back in Florida. They had to show me how to make hotdogs; we did not have that in Florida. I made some more friends working there, only to find out some went to the same high school. At some point, I started to steal again, eating food and not paying for it. That led to bigger things; I mean, we would take cases of meat and bread home. I was on the closing shift, and it was easy once the manager would go to the back office to count the money. My co-worker and I would load his car up with cases of food. Then it became a habit of stealing and playing dumb. At home, our refrigerator would be full of hamburger patties and bags of French fries. In between that, I befriended a kid in the neighborhood who was stealing from the neighbors. I fell into that as well; he and I would break into their apartments through the sliding glass door. We would search for money in every room, going through all the drawers, closets, and checking all the pockets. We stole from a lady who knew both of us. She would tell us she thought she had put the money away, but it went missing. She was second-guessing herself, wondering if she had put the money where she thought she hid it. The next time we got into her apartment, we found the money hidden in a different place. It must have been three to four hundred dollars. We took that money and went to the bowling alley and to the game room at the mall and had fun. We ate well; I mean, we had a good old time. It wasn't even a thought about the lady we stole from. We saw her a few days later, and she was very upset, crying and very emotional. "I know I put money away and it's not there," she said. "I don't know what's going on for my money to disappear like this. Something is going on; someone must have a key to my apartment. It must be one of the maintenance employees going inside unauthorized," she said. But I knew it was the sliding door; it was unlocked all the time. We would just climb up on the balcony and walk right in. She went to the rental office accusing them of taking money and going inside her apartment without authorization. They had no records of any work orders to be inside her place, and they denied any involvement. I looked at this woman in her face and knew it was me; I was the reason for her pain. Money that she worked for, and I stole it to have fun. Again, I don't know why I was doing things like that. I didn't say anything to her, but I never stole from her again. Not long after, we had to move again, far away from my school bus stop and work. I didn't want to leave the area; it wasn't even four months, and we were moving again. I decided to ask my uncle if I could live with him. I did not want to switch schools again. He said OK vocally, but in his heart, hell no. It seemed to start off OK; I did not have my own room, I slept on the floor in the living room or den. Within a few weeks, things started to change in the household with him. I was working and going to school with football practice in between. Coming in late in the evening, I guess, was not particularly the agreement. I really tried as much as possible not to be a burden to them, not to eat too much food or run up any water or light bills for them. I was just looking for a place to crash at night and then go to my mom's house for the weekend. But attitudes began to show that he did not want me there. Everything I did was a problem. I tried helping around the house — cutting the grass, taking the trash out, and giving him money when I got paid. Either the grass wasn't cut right, or if he would get home before I did, he'd say, "You didn't take out the garbage. You're not giving me enough money," he said. I was in a bad place all around. My grades dropped, and when that happened, I was ineligible to play football. I was able to participate in practice but not in the games. It was a truly short stay. Because of the tension, he said it would be best to go back to my mom's house. I did not care anymore!

My grades were bad anyway, and my friend was back in Florida. At this point, my mindset was whatever. I moved back in with my mom across town, no more school for me, and I quit Wendy's. I hung out around the new apartment complex for a while; we all were missing Florida. She decided to move back. She sold everything for the move. Only this time, my brother was not coming with us right away. We did not move back to West Palm Beach, but to Perrine, Florida, an hour and a half away from West Palm Beach. This time, we moved in with my auntie, my uncle's ex-wife, and her two kids. Right out of the gate, tension was there. To this very day, I do not know why she said yes. She just should have said no when mom asked if we could live with them. She really did not want us there; she would say things to us often like, "My bills are going up, water, lights." My mom was giving her some money, but not enough. I would eat small portions of food and still be hungry most nights. Shit, I was a growing teenager. Plus, I decided to drop out of school in the ninth grade. I figured, what the hell! When I told mom I wasn't going back to school, she said, "OK, don't worry about it. Momma didn't finish either, and I'm doing fine." I wasn't going to have stability anyway. So, I found the closest Wendy's and got the job right away. It was the only thing I knew how to do. The tension grew, and mom and auntie got into a big argument, with auntie having the upper hand. We were in her house, and she was in charge. She put us out, and thank God my cousin opened her apartment to us temporarily. We lived there for a few months, and I continued to work. Sleeping on the floor was not fun at all. I felt out of place when it came to the petty things like turning on the TV or going into the kitchen to fix something to eat. I just wanted to stay out of the way as much as possible. My auntie would come by and say to my cousin, "I wouldn't let their asses stay with you. They are not your responsibility. You don't have room for them," which would make my mom fire back at her with a variety of curse words back and forth. After that, we had to get back to West Palm Beach and get my brother from Texas back to Florida. My uncle would come from Pahokee, Florida, to get us for the weekend, and somehow, I got myself over to West Palm Beach on one of those weekend days. I had to find my best friend, Tavis. Up until then, I hadn't seen him in two years. He didn't even know I had moved out of the state and that my last name had changed. My uncle helped me go on the hunt. I went to the last place I knew he had lived, but they had moved by then. I started knocking on some of the neighbors' doors, asking if anyone knew where they had moved. I finally found one of Tavis's friends who knew where they had moved to. His parents allowed him to come with me and my uncle to show me. Man, he took us right to the house. I knocked on the door, and when it opened, I saw his mom sitting on the sofa. I didn't even wait for them to say, "Come in." I just bust in like the SWAT team. It was a breath of fresh air when we saw each other. Nothing but love and hugs — I damn near cried. Had I known I would have found Tavis, I would have brought my stuff and not left. We had a lot to catch up on, and I didn't want to leave, but I had to. From that point, I was determined to get back home to West Palm Beach. Mom finally made it back too for a visit to find some of her friends, and she found one of her girlfriends from back in the day. We met up at her house, only to find out one of her kids had passed away in a house fire that started from a Christmas tree. Man, that hurt! I remember hanging out with her when our parents would go out on the town, and I would spend the night over there or vice versa. After living in Perrine for six months, it was time to go. We came back to West Palm Beach, only to move in with the same friend. My mom's friend opened her house to us until we found a place of our own. It was crowded, but I didn't care. I was home. One of the first things I did was go back to the same Wendy's where it all started and work full-time. I got back in immediately; it was like I never left. Once again, back living with someone, I could feel the tension starting, and now as a growing boy, I was starting to understand. Tavis's mom helped us find a place to live, and the remarkable thing about that was it was right down the street from them. I decided not to enroll back in school—what was the point? Tavis must have been in the tenth or eleventh grade, so we would have to hook up most days after school or work. He was smarter than me when it came to school. My boy was on it; his mom made sure of that.

I mean, he already had his driver's license, and here I was, driving without one. Lol. I always had to take the back roads to avoid the police. He made me step up my game to get what I needed to be on the up and up. Life went on, and I continued to bring home the check and give it to my mom. In frustration, I got tired of walking or catching the city bus to and from work. I remember riding the bus up and down Broadway, seeing all the car lots everywhere. I didn't understand what "buy here, pay here" meant. Some cars had different amounts on the windshield with money down or weekly payments. I decided to get my first car no matter what with the next check. I had no license, so my brother put the car in his name. We walked up and down Broadway looking. My check was three hundred and fifty dollars. I found a maroon Chevrolet Chevette. I was ecstatic; the car was two-tone. I had no insurance, not that I knew what that meant. All I knew was my payment was fifty dollars a week, and I was rolling. That was the beginning of some independence and the momentum I needed. Things were going in the right direction again. Mom was surprised and mad that I didn't give her my check. Once I bought a car, I wanted to buy more things and fix up the car. It felt great being able to come and go as I pleased without waiting for a ride via bus, taxi, or walking. I still have a picture of me standing next to the car at seventeen. It was not long after Tavis got his first car too. Once that happened, we would meet up on the weekend at the car wash. Cleaning them inside and out, we had them looking good and smelling good for the ladies. We would get dressed—I mean, we would get fresh, clean clothes on, a fresh haircut brushed to the side like New Edition. That is who Tavis thought we were: New Edition. Before our cars, this fool would have me walking down the street singing "Cool It Now" (lol). Heading to the mall, not to buy anything, but just to walk around to be seen by the ladies. And we made sure they knew we had our own cars. None of the tires matched—four different brand tires (lol)—because we didn't have the money to buy new ones. We bought used ones and only got them when one went bad. Tavis and I had a saying whenever we had to borrow each other's cars. We would say, "Let me tell your ass something before I put my keys in your hand. If you get into an accident, do not come back. Just get on I-95 and keep going. I do not want to hear this 'I got hurt' shit. Just get on the highway and start walking or clawing—just do not ever come back. Keep going" (lol). One night, I went to bed early. I was tired, and when I woke up the next morning, I got dressed to leave, grabbed the keys, and walked outside—only to find my car was not there. In a panic, I ran back inside. "Mom, my car is gone!" I was crying because I did not know what had happened to my car. "Someone stole my car!" I said to her. She came outside and saw the same thing, but let me tell you, she knew what happened. She got down like she was Columbo himself. She woke my brother up and asked where my car was. He went into the denial stage. "I don't know why you're asking me about the car. I don't know." "Ernest, stop lying!" she said. "I know you know where the car is. I'm going to ask you again." He then started crying. "I got it last night. I wanted to go for a ride, and the car broke down at the high school in the city." The thing was, my car was a 6-speed manual, and he did not know how to drive a manual. He had burnt the clutch and left it parked, then walked back home. I had gone to bed that night like every other night, putting my keys on top of the dresser, not knowing he would sneak into my room to get the keys and drive off. He put the keys back where he got them, like nothing ever happened. Before I knew it, I could not hold back the tears; I burst out crying. My emotions overwhelmed me uncontrollably. Mom had a mechanic friend and asked him if he could help. We went down to the school, and sure enough, there it was, sitting in the parking lot. I teared up again, but he assured me he was going to fix it. It took about two months for him to fix my car. You see, he was one of those backyard mechanics, but he was a good one. Once my car was fixed, from that moment on, I slept with my keys inside my underwear that I was wearing to bed. I got a deadbolt lock and installed it on the bedroom door. I would wake up in the middle of the night just to check if my car was still there. I was paranoid. I was growing weary of Wendy's and wanted more. There must be more to life. I started stealing from them. I would take money out of the register every day. Whenever you needed to void something off the customer's order, the manager was supposed to come over with his or her manager key to do it. There was one manager, when you needed a void, he would hand you the key to do it yourself. It can't be that easy. I mean, this manager was lazy and sloppy looking. I don't think he cared at all. I took the key one night to make a void; the manager was in the back office, chilling, I guess. I voided almost two hundred dollars' worth of food. I took the money from the drawer and gave him the key back. The next day, I showed up for work like normal. I was working the mid-shift, and the police walked in. I thought they were coming in for lunch, but they came behind the counter and went to the back.

The next thing I knew, an officer grabbed me and took me to the back. I was scared as hell. They showed me a report that the other manager had run, which showed all the voids from my register. I was caught. I still had some of the money in my pocket. They put my ass in handcuffs, told me my Miranda rights, and walked me right out the door. Past all my other coworkers and customers. They put me in the patrol car and took me to jail. I got fingerprinted and had my picture taken. I had a mugshot. They put me in a cell, and I was there for a few hours. Somehow, they got hold of my mom to get me out. She was more upset that she had to get me versus me stealing. I had to go back to Wendy's to get my car. I jumped out of my mom's car quickly, hoping no one would see me. As quickly as I could, I walked fast to my car, got in, and took off like I had robbed a bank. I was glad they did not have my car towed away, but they pressed charges. They wanted the money back. When I went to court, I pled guilty to all charges. The judge took it easy on me. I had to pay back the money I stole and do 50 hours of community service. I served my community service at the local basketball gym, the same gym where Tavis and I took karate. I had to sweep the floors, take out the trash, and pick up unused basketballs. Do you think I learned my lesson? My ex-coworker from Wendy's was now working at a local convenience store/gas station that paid two dollars more an hour. I jumped on it right away; I already had customer service and cashiering experience. I started on the morning shift at 7 a.m. The owner was nice to all her employees; she allowed us to eat whatever we wanted in the store if we worked that day. If you needed gas, you could get it and write it on a gas slip to pay on Friday. Once I was fully trained, I took the midnight shift, 11 p.m. to 7 a.m. It wasn't long before I started doing things I was not supposed to. I started giving food and gas away and pocketing the money — selling cigarettes and beer from the inventory on a regular basis and pocketing the money. Every shift, I had to make a money drop in the floor safe inside the booth at the end of the shift. The safe had a slot on the side like a mailbox. Only the owner had the key to open the main door. One night, somehow, I stumbled upon opening the door without the key by taking the fuse out. I would take money from the other shifts a couple of times a week. I started fixing up my car with stolen money — paint job, stereo system, tinted windows. I mean, you could hear me coming from two blocks away. Taking gas without writing a gas slip — I mean, I got loose. They knew something was wrong but could not figure out how or who. This went on for a little while. I remember showing up for my shift, and the supervisor met me outside and said the owner said that I could not work tonight. She said, "Come back first thing tomorrow morning, the owner wants to talk to me." I said, "If I cannot work tonight, I'm not coming back." I got into my car and drove off. Damn! NOW WHAT! No job. I messed it up again for myself. The owner was good to me, and I did not do right by her. She did not deserve that; I was only concerned about myself—pride and hardheadedness. I must have taken three to five thousand when it was all said and done. Tavis was getting ready to leave for the Army. I had to find a job right away. You would have thought I would have paid for the car with all that stolen money, but I still had to make that weekly payment. I got a job at a furniture store warehouse, pulling furniture out of the steel, staging it in bays by zip codes for deliveries, and getting my first experience and training driving a forklift in a big warehouse. This was quite different for me. I got to know the general manager and supervisor well. They taught me how things are done, showed me the ropes, and trusted me. I did so well pulling merchandise and working hard that I was offered an office position because an employee was moving on to something else. The office job was confirming customers' orders. The customer would go into the sales floor and pick out what they wanted, and the orders would come to me for processing. Once confirmed, the customer would drive up to the bay door and show a receipt for proof of purchase. The new forklift driver would get the order and load it onto the truck for them. I got good at the office position. Pulling orders out of the racks was once my job, so processing became extremely easy. I went with the flow until I started stealing again. Lots of customers would come to pick up their own merchandise to avoid delivery and setup fees. I saw how easy it was for the customer to ride up and back into the bay door and hand an employee a receipt without any supervisor or member of management checking paperwork. This was truly a trusting company, and like before, I started taking advantage of the system that was in place. I had to find someone that would go in with me — someone who wanted extra cash too, undercover. When I found that coworker, he and I started to plot and plan how to make this work. If we had people who wanted modern furniture for a good deal, we could do it ourselves and make money. All they would have to do was go onto the showroom floor and pretend they wanted something with a salesperson. The buyer had to wait for the salesperson to go away and get the SKU number from the tag on the furniture for what they wanted. I would print up an old receipt from someone else's old order, then give it to them while I looked it up on the computer for the location of that specific piece of furniture in the warehouse. My coworker would go pull it. It was a foolproof plan and money maker for us. We would split the money 50/50. Once we found a customer, it was like clockwork, just as planned. We were nervous as hell, right up until the $3,000 in cash hit our hands. I mean, it was too easy. We pulled it off and wanted to do it again. We waited a few weeks to see if anything was noticed by management. Absolutely nothing. The first person we stole merchandise for told someone else, and then orders started to roll in faster than we could keep up with. All cash — no checks or money orders. This went on for a few months. It was not until the legitimate customers showed up for a pickup, and other pullers went to locations in the racks that the computer said it would be, and it would not be there. Unbeknownst to us, they were alert — something was wrong. They knew that much furniture could not be missing from all those locations the system said it should be. I am talking about bedroom sets, living room sets, dining room sets, wall units, and mattresses — all missing. Every aisle had a number, and every level had a letter. That is how you could tell what location each piece of furniture was located. Just as they had pullers, they also had pluggers. That meant the employee would unload the trucks coming in from the receiving department, coming from the factory. As they unloaded the trucks, the pluggers would place the furniture in the racks and write the locations of placements on SKU cards. After the trucks were unloaded, they would turn in all the cards into the office for keying. On the day my coworker got caught, the fake customer pulled up like always and handed him the fake receipt. Except this time, a supervisor came up and stood by the bay door, waiting for him to come back with the furniture. He saw the supervisor standing there waiting, and he (my coworker) started riding around on the forklift, pretending to look for the furniture. After he could not play it off any longer, he came up front, and the supervisor took the receipt and went into the office to get on the phone for verification. We both were scared as hell, him more than I; he was the one with the fake receipt and dealing with the people at the bay door. He gave the fake customer the signal to leave because something was wrong. I remember the supervisor taking him into the smaller office, and I could see them through the window. I could not imagine what was being said. I was not sure if he was telling everything or keeping quiet. My heart was racing a thousand miles an hour. To my surprise, he took the fall without telling them I was involved. He got fired and was escorted out of the building. I do not think charges were filed for all the missing furniture. We must have made $25k each by the time the gig was up, and again, no one ever suspected me of any involvement. With that much cash in hand, an 18-year-old in the late '80s, again, I was riding nice, dressed to kill, looking good, smelling good, all by breaking trust with the company and the people helping me with opportunities. A brief time later, the company went out of business, and if I had to guess, it was from other thefts also. By that time, I had a baby girl with no income, and my girlfriend's dad was tough and did not play. He helped with the baby but made it truly clear that it was my baby and my responsibility. It got worse as the weeks and months passed. No income and no car — it all got repossessed. Back in the same old cycle, walking or taking the bus to and from places I wanted to be. Even the furniture I stole for my mom, she sold to one of her friends who did not pay all the money. I was mad as hell — she stole merchandise from us and did not pay for it. Who does she think she is? Where is my money? I went by her house several times to collect payment, and she did not have it. Seeing my stolen sofa sitting in her living room, looking so sweet and lovely, I wanted my money, but common sense kicked in. How can I get mad about something I stole, then someone stole it from me? We had to move again. I remember the landlord coming to collect the rent — a nice guy too. He knocked on the door, and I let him in. Mom was sitting on the chair smoking a cigarette, and she let him have it. "I do not have any damn money!" she said. "Shit, I don't need you to come here asking me about rent; I'm just going to move out." He politely said, "OK," and went on his way. This was a nice little house too, but we had to move. We moved into a two-bedroom apartment next to a drug house. People were coming and going all day long. I was fifteen miles away from my girlfriend and baby with no transportation. I started hanging out with the next-door neighbor's son. We started doing things that we should not have. Back then, there were lots of empty houses with window air conditioning. We would break into the empty houses and steal the ACs to sell them to whomever. By this time, the water was off again, and my back was against the wall. Having to go next door on the regular and ask to fill a bucket with water to flush the toilet again was embarrassing. Having to pee or poop with one or two days of poop already in the toilet was horrible. Some days were better than others, with no food, waiting on Mom to bring something home later that day. I tried to find work every day. Back then, you had to get the local newspaper and look in the wanted ads for jobs. No phone in the house or cell phone existed for the common folk, so I walked where I could all over West Palm Beach looking for work. I must have gone down to the city every week trying to get hired. I spoke to the supervisor face-to-face on a regular basis, asking him for a chance to prove myself. He would say, "Come back next week," and I did for a while until the light finally came on. He is not going to give me an opportunity, but I would get there at 6 a.m. in the morning just like I was an employee, ready to start work wherever they needed me. Park and recreation, garbage truck, or on the main street digging holes or fixing holes—I did not care; I just needed income for my baby and to help with the water bill. Since he didn't hire me, I took a job with the PGA International Resort in the banquet setup. I went through the day of orientation. They had a café for employees to eat lunch on them, just as long as you worked that day. I started work the next day, and let me tell you, it was crazy in that department. I got there, and they had something like four hundred tables to set up and a thousand chairs. Halfway through the setup, the supervisor stopped the team to rearrange the setup. That was hard work that I'd never done. Racks and racks of tables and racks and racks of chairs. The racks of tables must have had fifty tables, and the racks of chairs were twenty high or so. That was my second day and my last day. I didn't go back. I was sore as I could be, rolling that many tables and chairs for a party. I couldn't see myself doing that every day. The Lord knows I needed the money, but no, I was not doing that. I started walking around looking again, and on days I was not walking looking for work, I would go to the public library and hang out there all day, just so I could use a clean toilet when needed. The library also had a popcorn machine; the popcorn was free, so I ate popcorn for breakfast and lunch. The daily paper was available, and I would go through the wanted ads looking for work. Once my neighbor moved out of the apartment next door, I broke into it just to use the bathroom at night. I broke in through the bedroom window to poop and pee for a while. When the city finally turned the water off, I used the toilet until it was full, then I peed and pooped in the tub. I did not care; it was the next-door apartment. Somehow, I thought it would be a promising idea to let my girlfriend and daughter come live with me. I guess she and her parents were clashing.

Here I was, without any income or a stable place to live, and they moved in with us. My mom did not care; it was fun at first having my kid and lady with me. But the dark side was coming, the three of us sleeping in the room on top of a mattress on the floor. We both just tried to make the best of it. Her dad knew it would not last for long, that she'd be back in a few weeks or a month. I could not buy my child anything, not even diapers, baby wipes, milk, or baby food. I was down for the count; I had to tap out and send her back to her parents until I figured it out. The same middle school friend who helped me get a job with Wendy's got me in with a security company working at the front gate of a senior citizen community. I was working the 3 p.m. to 11 p.m. shift. The job was about ten miles away. Man, did I struggle getting to and from work every damn day. It was extremely boring working there at the security gate. It was an easy job but boring. All I did was wait for visitors to drive up. I would write down their names and what unit they were visiting. I did not last long working there because we had to move again because we got evicted. We had nowhere to go. Mom asked someone she knew if she could put our things in her house until she found a place.

We put almost everything inside this lady's house, and mom moved into a motel on Broadway. This motel was owned and run by people from India. The motel was like a small one-bedroom apartment. The owners lived up front. Their office and living quarters were all in one. You had to walk past their office window to get to your apartment. They saw everyone who was coming and going. Someone from the family would always be sitting in the window. And if you needed something, you had to ring the bell for service. You had to pay rent weekly, every Monday by 8 a.m. The more people that lived in each unit, the more money you had to pay. You were allowed to have visitors until 5 p.m.; after that, all visitors had to leave. By this time, my brother had been in jail for a while, so it was just mom and me. Come to find out, I was a visitor; she was only paying for herself to live there. I was working the 3 p.m. to 11 p.m. shift, so I was gone by 1:30 p.m., walking or catching a cab to work.

Every night, I had to figure out how I was going to get back to the motel. I either walked, or one of my co-workers would drop me off if they were going in that direction. I would have them drop me off a block away so I would not be noticed by the owners, sneaking in and out of there trying not to get caught by a family member from the front office. To pull this off, I had to come in from the back alley at 1 a.m. in the morning and jump over the concrete wall. Quickly and quietly, I'd tap on the window or door so mom could let me in, hoping she was not sleeping too hard to hear me knocking, or someone from the office could hear me tapping on the window. Once in, I would take a shower and go to bed for a few hours. I had to be up and out by 6 a.m. and come back around 8:30 a.m. just to look like a visitor. The office opened at 7 a.m. I had to walk around the streets until then.

When I got back, I would go back to bed for a few more hours of sleep before it was time to get out again. Even now, thinking back, it makes me mad that I went through that shit. One night, I got there like normal, ducking and dodging the owners. I did not know what was going on with Mom, but when I came in, she opened the door, and the look she gave me was off. She did not even say hi, like I had done something or owed her some money. I got out of the shower, went to bed, and she started going off, talking aloud to herself, loud enough for me to hear. "I do not know how much longer I am going to let his ass come here," she said. "I have to take care of my goddamn self, and he is going to get me put out. Shit, he's sneaking in here every motherfucking night. You need to take care of your motherfucking self!" I mean, she went on and on for a good thirty minutes. It got so bad, I just got up, got dressed, grabbed all my stuff at 2 a.m. in the morning, and left. I came out of the room, and she was sitting on the couch, smoking a cigarette, looking mad as hell. We made eye contact, and I walked out the front door and back over the wall. I didn't know where I was going, but I left.

Here I was, an eighteen-year-old Black male walking down Broadway with two bags of clothing and personal shit in tow. I had no idea where I was going; I just started walking. I walked towards my girlfriend's house, eleven miles away. Scared and unsure what to do, something popped up in my head to go to a friend of mine's house, thirteen miles away. I remember he lived with his grandma, and she had rooms for rent. I had to walk through an unbelievably bad part of town to get there. I walked fast, looking straight ahead. I was very tired when I got there.

Here I was at 4 a.m. in the morning, knocking on his bedroom window. I told him what was going on and that I needed a place to stay for a while. He let me in and gave me a room for the night. I was able to speak to his grandma the next morning, and she allowed me to stay. I got the rules of the house and how much I had to pay every two weeks. My mom had me in a tough situation. I do not think she really cared if I was dead or alive; all I knew was she put my ass out. I thank God I had a job to pay rent and help with the baby. What a relief it was for his grandma to say yes, I could live there, because she did not know me at all. She did not ask me any questions about why Mom put me out. I'm assuming my friend told her the situation, I guess. I did not ask to eat there or anything extra. I wanted to be sure not to be in the way. If I was in my room, I was incredibly quiet. I just needed a roof over my head without ducking and dodging anyone. It was a nice little room, too; I fixed it up the way I wanted it, and it was not too far from my girlfriend's house. I still struggled to and from places. My girlfriend's dad really helped me a lot with getting to work. He knew I was doing my best to help with the baby; they were living with him, and he saw my baby more than I did. He did not try to take over; he wanted to help us, and again, he made sure I understood that it was my responsibility. Most days, if I were not at work or the weekends, he would let me hang out at his house with his family. I was able to wash my clothes and get a home-cooked meal a few times a week. I did not see my mom for a few months; I was taking it one day at a time. Something kept me going, something inside was driving me not to feel sorry for myself. I did not know what the future held in store for me. I lived there for a while, but I could not seem to get ahead. There must be something more to life than what I have seen and experienced.

I met a Florida State Trooper who gave me some information about becoming a Trooper. Man, did that catch my attention, but I had one problem: I did not finish high school. He said you must have a high school diploma to be considered for the job. By that time, Tavis was serving in the army. I really did not have anyone to lean on or talk to either. I hid my pain well, with a smile on my face. I do not think I cried, but in deep thought, I did not talk to God, but somehow, I think He was talking to me. The security job was fading fast. I had no car, and the job was not motivating, nor were there any real opportunities. And if they gave me the opportunity, I would have messed that up too. I quit! Now, what was I going to do? I still had to pay rent for my room, I still had to eat, and I still had a baby to take care of.

Something led me back to Wendy's. Wendy's, where it all started. The same Wendy's that hired me back when I came back from Texas. The same Wendy's I stole from and was escorted out in handcuffs. They hired me back like nothing ever happened. I needed the income; I wasn't ashamed at all. I made the decision to do it right this time. I thought I would move my way up to shift leader and then to manager. I stayed straight this time doing my job. I was going above and beyond with my customer service skills. I was on time for work, taking any shift that was available, trying to get out of the hole. I felt right at home and loved what I was doing.

CHAPTER 4

Behind Wendy's was a construction crew putting the final touches on a business called Costco Wholesale. I had no idea what that was. Once Costco opened, a lot of the employees would come over to Wendy's for lunch. I mean, that place was a zoo. All I saw were people going in and out all day long, fighting for parking, and baskets full of big boxes and food. I was working hard and putting in all the hours I could.

After a few months, one of the managers who came in all the time came over to my register and asked me if I knew what Costco was. I said, "No ma'am, I think it must be some kind of store or something." She said, "It's a wholesale membership club where people pay to come in and shop." It still didn't make any sense to me—hell, I was on my way up at Wendy's! She said, "I've been watching you for a while, and I've noticed how hard you're working and how nice you treat the customers. I'd like you to come work for us." I said, "I'm not leaving Wendy's. I'm on my way up to shift leader. I'm making this my career." She said, "That's great you want a career, but I'd still like you to come work for us. Costco is a great company, and it has lots of opportunities for you." I was making about five dollars and fifty cents an hour at Wendy's. She said, "We have a distribution center that just opened not too far from here, and I want to get you there." I asked, "How much does it pay?" She said, "We start everyone at eight dollars and fifteen cents an hour." Eight dollars an hour! With all she said, all I heard was eight dollars an hour. Three more dollars an hour — wow! "Yes ma'am, I would like to give it a shot." The next day, she came into Wendy's with the application for me to fill out. It was one sheet, front and back. I completed the application and gave it back to her the next day. I remember putting my pager and Wendy's number on the application for them to reach out to me.

It wasn't a week later when I got the call to come in for the interview. The management introduced themselves to me, and I got the rundown on what the company was all about. Once I got through the process, I got hired, and I was excited. They told me to report to work at 6 a.m., and let me tell you, I was late on my very first day. That was the first job I had with an early start like that. I woke up at 5:45 a.m., and my heart was jumping out of my chest. I walked through the door at 6:30, thinking about what I was going to say to them. The manager said, "You're late." I played stupid and said, "I am?" He said, "Yes, you are. We said to be here at 6 a.m." I replied, "Oh, I thought you said to be here at 6:30. My apologies, I must have heard you wrong, sir." I was lying through my teeth. At nineteen years old, this was the most money I'd ever made. They sat me down and went over the company handbook, the dos and don'ts, the benefits, and what that meant. And how much money I could be making in a few years—I did not want to mess up this wonderful opportunity. I would be classified as part-time, guaranteed 21 hours a week with the potential to work more hours as the business picked up. Seeing everything was based on seniority, the senior employees got everything first—more hours, days off, brand-new equipment, and first in line for any promotions. I started working and was assigned to the receiving department, learning how to count merchandise from a delivery.

My trainer seemed like he didn't want to train me. He wasn't giving me all the information I needed or was going so fast through the steps on purpose. By that time in my life, I had picked up a few skills on my own. I was a better reader and more outspoken; I knew he was not training me correctly from the get-go. I had trained lots of people at Wendy's, and he was off just by his attitude. The man would not even look me in the eyes when he was talking to me. I do not know why; he and I did not know each other. I had to nip it in the bud quickly before something jumped off between us. This was the job I did not want to mess up. I started asking more questions just to get him to train me right. "Hey man, what is up? Why do you have such an attitude towards me? It's like your stuff doesn't stink. Or you're truly short with your answers. I didn't do anything to you. Either you train me right, or I will go to the manager."

I was talking to a wall; he did not change much. He treated other employees the same way. So, I pushed myself to learn on my own or from someone else who was willing to help me. I learned all I could and was rocking the house. The managers saw how well I was doing and decided to train me on the forklift. I had not been on that type of forklift before, but here I go. They put my ass in the shipping department. Here is where I really honed in on my skills and abilities. Once I understood how to stack freight, how weight and cubic feet worked, I was able to load trucks. I had to make sure the weight was distributed correctly on the trailers, filling it up from top to bottom, from front to back. I was a loading machine; it took me thirty minutes to load a truck while it took the senior employees an hour. But the twenty hours a week were killing me.

My check was not that much more than Wendy's because I was full time there. But I had to hang in there and be patient. I had to make it to the top scale that Costco paid — fourteen dollars and seventeen cents an hour. You see, the more hours you worked at Costco, the faster you got your raises until you topped out. My manager was a tough, hard-nosed, straight-to-the-point person. He treated everyone fairly and held everyone to the same standards. He expected you to be on time and work hard. He would walk up and down the dock, making sure everyone was working. And if you weren't working, standing around talking, Lord have mercy, he would tear you up. Nothing disrespectful, but he went in on you. He pushed you to be your best, and he wanted a good hard day's work from everyone. Things began to change again for me on the positive side. In the beginning, they made sure you were working twenty-one hours a week, only four hours a day. It wasn't very encouraging, but I saw the big picture, the finish line where I needed to reach.

After a few butt chewings from my manager, which made me push myself, he saw the improvements before I did. He started asking me to stay longer on my shift. He would say, "Son, I know you are only scheduled for 4 hours today, but can you stay all day?" I sure can. Little by little, I started getting more hours. I was still scheduled for twenty-one hours a week but was working around thirty-six hours. Some of the other employees that started with the company at the same time I did not get the same offer. You see, they thought that the manager was mean and always on them. Or they tried pushing back in some form or fashion. Not me. All that I've been through and am still going through, I refused to mess this up. I know I didn't deserve any of the blessings that had been coming my way, but they were coming.

The next thing I knew, I was making twelve dollars an hour, and I got promoted to full-time, guaranteed forty hours a week. Man, I was on my way. I was still living with different people at the time. I was taking care of my lady and my baby. I had a used car to get me back and forth, honest money in my pocket, and was doing okay. This was it. I wanted my own place, the place where I was in charge — my own, my own, my own, my own. I knew the apartment complex I had in mind.

Here I was, twenty-one years old. I walked into the leasing office with my head held high and said, "Hi, I would like to rent an apartment." "Sir, you need to fill out an application first," they said. "Application!" Oh, I was not aware of that. "Here is the application. Please fill it out and return it to us. There will be a fifty-dollar application fee, a twenty-five-dollar credit check fee, along with a three-hundred-dollar security deposit and the first month's rent."

The application asked for past places that I lived in, and they needed the landlord's information too. Well, I did not have any of that. I explained that this was my first time living on my own. I had no references other than my friend's grandmother, but the office manager was incredibly supportive. She saw that I had been working at Costco for almost two years and had a steady income. I needed nine hundred dollars to move in if everything came back on the up and up. Well, it did! I was approved for my first place. I was so happy and excited. It was like life could not get any better than this. It really didn't hit me until they put the keys in my hands. I walked over to it and into an empty place. I had no furniture at all, only the clothes on my back. I didn't care. I had my place. What a relief it was.

That feeling was amazing. Because I had only my clothes, I made that my bed to sleep on. Yes, that's right. I piled them up on the floor like a sleeping bag and slept on that for a while. Then I heard about places where you could rent furniture and make low weekly payments. Anything you needed for your house, they had. All they required was for the customers to have a job and five references. Hell, that was right up my alley; I did not have a big bank account. I met their requirements, and the first thing I got was a bedroom set and a small TV. The payments were thirty-five dollars a week for ninety-five weeks. These places were called rent-to-own; after the weeks were fulfilled, it was yours.

As time went on, I would add more things to the account to fill my apartment, and of course, the more things, the more money, and more weeks were added. If your payment was due on a Friday and you missed it, Saturday morning they would blow your phone up calling you about the payment. If you happened to miss them calling you, they would show up to your house Monday morning demanding the money or merchandise. You could have been in the hospital sick, and they didn't care. They were gangsters with it too. I continued to work hard to keep the momentum going. After a few months, my girlfriend and daughter moved in; my own family was in the making. Because of my hatred for lights and water being turned off and moving all the time, I wanted to make damn sure I would never put them through that foolishness.

That was the first thing I would do when I got paid: pay my bills, buy groceries for the house, and whatever money was left, was left. If my bills were paid and food was in the house, I was content. My girlfriend's dad was a preacher, and he and his wife felt we were shacking up, living together but not married. They would say this made us look bad to the church. Especially his wife — she was more worried about their image than our walk with God. You see, she was mean as hell, and she was almost evil. It was not that I didn't want to get married; it was the way they came across. Her mom was the one who tried to convince me to give my daughter their last name, not mine. She would not even allow me to go inside the delivery room for her birth; she went.

At the time, I fell for the okey-doke and did not push back. I had allowed her to do that to me because I wanted to be respectful to them. I let her mom talk us into a couple of abortions; I would have had three kids by that time. But not this time. Even though my girlfriend's dad was extremely helpful, I was solid. I was going to do it on my own terms. You see, I loved her tremendously. We continued shacking up for a while, and day by day, we grew closer. I was able to fix up my daughter's room and make it all cute and girly for her. That made me want to work even harder, making sure she didn't want for anything. Before I knew it, I was topped out, making fifteen dollars an hour with full benefits for my family. It wasn't long before my lady was pregnant again. We were so excited. This would have been my fourth baby if we had them all. I decided to ask her to marry me.

It was the right thing to do, and the right time. By the time we had married, she was five months pregnant. Here she is, walking down the aisle of the church with a pop belly, wobbling in her white dress, on the arm of her dad. It was something special. We had 9 bridesmaids and 9 groomsmen. It was a big wedding, and lots of people were there. Watching my little girl walk down ahead of her mom, throwing flowers on the floor like we were from the nation of Zamunda. After the ceremony, we partied like it was 1999. We did not have money for a honeymoon, but we spent the night in a hotel on the beach overlooking the ocean.

CHAPTER 5

The next morning, we went home and back to work, getting the room set up for my new baby and buying what was needed for both. I was going into the delivery room this time, and what an experience it was. They brought the baby out—now I had two baby girls and a wife. I was doing it up. It felt good taking care of my family, making good money and all. I did so well at work. The assistant manager got promoted to general manager and was relocating to Boston. He asked me to come over to his house for dinner one night. I did not know what for—I knew we would hang out sometimes after work, playing basketball or just chilling. I got there and had dinner. He said, "You know I got promoted and am moving to Boston." "Yes, I know," I responded. He said, "I want you to come with me and grow with the company." I said, "Man, I do not know anything about Boston or even where it is. I will have to talk it over with my wife and get back to you." I went home thinking, Why me? Everything is going well for me here. I had to look at a map to see exactly where Boston was. I did not know what to do—I did not understand the opportunity or how far I could go with the company. By that time, Tavis was out of the service and working for Costco also. We both had our families started with our own apartments. This was a big decision. After talking to my wife and convincing Tavis to come with me, I went back to the manager with a yes—if Tavis could go. We were excited and scared at the same time. My mom had lived with us a few times, and my brother was in prison. We began to look at the area where the new depot was going to be and the area we wanted to live in. The ball was in motion. Tavis and I put our money together to rent one big U-Haul for both apartments. We continued to work and plan for the move, packing up things, etc. Before we knew it, it was time to go—I mean, the time flew by. The night before, we spent time with the families, having dinner, laughing, playing, and a whole lot of crying. Part of the plan was that Tavis would put his car on the trailer and drive the U-Haul halfway while I followed in my car, then we would switch. I had to leave my kids behind with my wife's parents. I wanted to get there safely, look around, find a place to live, and then send for them. It took us two days to get there, but we made it. My manager was already there— he was the one who hooked us up with a rental agency. They found us a one-bedroom efficiency apartment that we had to take. We all lived there for a while. It took every penny I had. After paying for the U-Haul, gas, first and last month's rent (without a lease), and then buying groceries for the house, I was broke until the next payday — not a dollar in my pocket after all that. We had to find a bigger spot to live and send for my kids. This was a challenge for us. We had no money, and all the apartments we were accustomed to had no availability. That was a long two weeks to go without any money in a new state and a new town. This was before GPS and cell phones. You see, it was easy driving from Florida to Boston — we just stayed on I-95 North all the way and followed the signs that read Boston. The town was different, nothing I had ever seen before. The trees were all assorted colors, and the houses had basements. We started work right away, getting the new depot prepared. The girls stayed home, and for a minute, I was living from check to check. Thank goodness the lights, water, and oil were included with the rent. You see, I came to realize that the oil was for the furnace in the basement to keep the building heated in the wintertime. Tavis was able to find an apartment in the next town over. Once he and his lady moved out, there was a little more room for me and my wife. As I continued to work, she continued to look for a bigger place to live.

On the weekends, we would venture out around town, learning about the area and people. We both started to miss our kids, especially her. It was taking a toll on her. I had to figure out how to make it happen fast. We saved up enough money over three months to move. She found a big house in the town of Woburn. The house was huge, with three levels and a basement. The place was so big that the attic could have been a room. But once we moved in, things started heading in the right direction. The owner lived behind us and was incredibly supportive. This time, we were responsible for all the utilities. I had heard that white people in Boston did not like Black people. Be careful around them, mind your manners. So, I was pumped up, watching and waiting for a white person to set me off — lol. But it was the opposite. We moved in, and the very next day, my next-door neighbor, an elderly white lady, knocked on my door. I had seen her as we moved in. She came over with a homemade loaf of bread, welcoming us to the neighborhood. I was so surprised and happy at the same time. She was genuinely nice to us and glad we were there. Five months or so had passed, and we sent for our kids. Her mom was going to fly up with them and stay with us for a few weeks. I was not too keen on seeing her mom, but I wanted my babies.

When they got there, we had their rooms ready and fixed up for them. Man, we were so happy to have our kids, and her mom was not as bad as I thought this time around. She was helpful, jumping in wherever we needed her to. It was cold as ice outside by this time — below five degrees or so. I noticed the inside of the house was starting to get colder. Again, I was new to this oil furnace thing. You see, the furnace pushed water through the pipes on the baseboard of the floor. Unbeknownst to me, I had the landlord come over to see what was going on—the furnace had run out of oil. This caused the water in the pipes to freeze. I had to turn the oven on with the door open to warm the house up. The landlord called for the oil company to come out to refuel the tank.

Once the tank was full, the landlord had to find exactly where the pipe had frozen, then take a blowtorch and wave it across the frozen part of the pipe to get the water circulating again. After an hour, the house began to warm up, and it came right on time because it began to snow—and snow heavily. It was a beautiful thing to see. The kids and I went outside and played in it. Before I knew it, you couldn't see your hand in front of your face—it was snowing so hard. Everything was white around us—a beautiful white too. It looked like God had opened a big bag of flour and dumped it over the city. It was cold as hell. It was so cold that we would blow bubbles in the air, and before they hit the ground, they were frozen. Man, this was not good old sunny South Florida at all. What a difference for us— all of us. Life was different. We had to meet new people and continue to learn our way around town. I got promoted to supervisor. This was something I did not see coming at all.

My manager saw my potential and hooked me up. I oversaw the receiving department, making sure trucks were processed and freight was run to the correct shipping lanes. I was doing well — opening a new depot was challenging for us. Tavis was the supervisor of the pallet department. After working, we would hang out with some of the locals and new employees — going out for a beer, playing basketball, or just chilling and getting to know each other. But then I started to miss home. I went into a bit of a slump. Between the cold and the unfamiliar area, I was bummed out. The people were fantastic, so I was able to maintain as best I could. My manager was very enthusiastic and encouraging. Again, there was someone who had plans for me, but I didn't see it. He worked hard to keep me focused on the bigger picture.

Unbeknownst to me, he planned a get-together at his house, inviting the crew that came up to Boston with us and a few new hires. He had food and drinks — you know, a small dinner party. Because I was in my feelings, I didn't go. The following Monday, he called me into his office and asked, "What happened? Why didn't you and your wife come to the get-together?" He said, "The get-together was for you, Baron." I said, "For me?" "Yes, for you, man," he replied. "I wanted to surprise you with another promotion and celebrate with everyone." He had promoted me from receiving supervisor to receiving manager. I had dropped the ball on him. I felt bad — how could I do that? I let my feelings get the best of me. I couldn't say anything but, "I'm sorry." They had a good time without me anyway, and it was for me. He said, "B, I'm with you, man, but you need to pull yourself together. Congratulations — I'm promoting you now. Let's go make the announcement to the employees." We went out onto the floor and stopped the entire building. All the employees gathered in the middle of the warehouse, and he made the announcement. I got applause, the key to the building, a pager, and a nice raise. I was taught a lot about management functions and more about the business side of the company. I put my feelings aside and focused.

CHAPTER 6

By then, my mom was struggling as usual, and my brother was locked up. Mom needed a place to stay. According to her, she was sleeping in the park. After talking to my wife, we decided to let her come live with us. My wife had started working as well, which would help us with babysitting costs—Mom could watch the kids while we were at work. So, I sent for her. Mom would have her own room and everything.

It started off okay—lol—but before long, tension flared up between Mom and my wife. Whatever the argument of the day was, it somehow ended up as "He is my son" or "He's my husband." I was caught in the middle, trying to keep the peace in the house. We had some good weeks and some bad ones. None of us had considered the pros and cons of her living with us. Mom also wanted us to keep her entertained.

Whenever my wife and I would go out to the movies or dinner, Mom felt she should be able to go too. But that wasn't the case—not even close. We felt we were already providing her with a place to live, food to eat, a few dollars in her pocket, and no bills to pay. In return, she was supposed to watch my kids while we were at work. When we got home from work, Mom would go for a walk down the street, mad at us. She would be huffing and puffing, mumbling under her breath. She decided to go back to New Jersey and get away from us for a while. She got herself a bus ticket and left. She gave us enough time to get our old babysitter back to watch the kids. We went on living and working throughout the year. Mom went back and forth to and from New Jersey. After going there a few times, she was able to find my dad — a man I knew nothing about, a man who, if he walked in front of me or passed me, I would not know who he was.

I remember her coming back and telling me, "I found your dad. I gave him your number, and he is going to call you soon." I did not know what to think at the time. What was I going to say when and if he called? I do not remember how the conversation went when he called, but I remember setting up the bus ticket to go down to meet him. I was twenty-three years old and met my dad for the first time.

My wife and I went, leaving the kids home with Mom. We took the Greyhound bus to New Jersey for a six-hour ride. We got off the bus at the station, and my heart was racing a thousand miles an hour. It must have been two hundred people walking around. I did not know what this man looked like; it was not like he was holding up a sign with my name on it. I was walking back and forth, up and down the corridor like a lost child. My wife knew I was nervous, and her bold ass saw an older man walking around looking like he was lost too.

From a distance, I saw her walk right up to him. They were talking. I saw her point her finger at me, then they started walking in my direction. She knew the situation. When we met, we introduced ourselves, shook hands, and gave each other a hug. As we were hugging, I looked over at my wife—she was crying hard. I mean, snot and tears were running out. She did all the crying for both of us because we did not shed a tear. It was like two lions from the same pride. He was my height and my skin tone, and we looked alike. We stayed for the weekend, with lots of small talk on the ride to his house.

When we got there, there was some more small talk. Come to find out, I had a stepmom and a baby sister. My sister looked just like me. She must have been about six years old—a little mini-me. Talk about softening up my heart. I did not call my dad by his name; I called him Dad. They had this big dinner prepared for me every night. He took us around town to meet more of the family, like Antwone Fisher. Just getting the chance to spend time with them and meeting everyone was nice. Dad and I did not get into the past right away. We just enjoyed the present time together. My wife was incredibly supportive, helping me stay relaxed given our time together. The weekend ended, and it went fast. And of course, we made plans right away to come back. Twenty-plus years and finally meeting my dad. We got home, and Mom wanted to know all about it.

Although it was awesome that she went and found him, there were too many unanswered questions that had to be answered at the right time. You cannot catch up on a two-day weekend for twenty-plus years of absence. I kept it simple and said to Mom, "It was good to meet him. Thank you." Work was going well. Tavis and I did our thing, along with the girls and kids on the weekend.

A year had passed. The business was growing fast, and we could not keep up with the demand. Suddenly, a meeting was called at work by our general manager. We were informed that our current location was not big enough for the business to grow. We were going to have to relocate to a bigger facility, and that facility was in New Jersey. New Jersey! Why New Jersey? We had just settled here, and now we had to move again. I did not see this coming at all. We were given a few options: we could stay here in Boston, and the company would place us in one of the local warehouses; we could move with the depot to New Jersey and continue to grow with the company; or we could resign and move on. I did not know what to do. By this time, my mom had moved back to Florida, and the kids were not old enough to start school. Tavis and I got together to decide what was best for us. Tavis was dead set on not moving—he would not budge at all. "B, I am not moving my family again," he said. "We just got here, we spent a lot of money to move here, and I am not doing that again. Not even for you, bro."

My best friend, my brother—bad boys for life—would not go with me. Tavis was able to take a position in a local Costco warehouse. I decided to move on without my brother and relocate to New Jersey. I was hurt and felt some type of way toward the GM. I had to hide my hurt inside; this was the beginning of the end for me. How was I going to pull this off without my brother? Although I had my own family and would be moving closer to my dad, I was still hurting. It wasn't like Dad and I were desperately looking to hang out every chance we had. As we prepared to move, one positive thing—so I thought—was that, as a manager, the company paid for the move. The movers would come, pack everything for us, load it, and take it to New Jersey. We had no idea where we were going to live. I had no money saved to pay first, last, and the security deposit that most people had to pay to move in.

CHAPTER 7

As the weeks passed and moving day got closer, I needed help with finances. The general manager stepped up to the plate to help me out—he put everything I needed on his credit card. He put my family in a hotel until I found a place. I found a storage place in New Jersey to put my things. The packers came a week prior to the moving truck arriving. Everything was packed and ready to go. The moving truck arrived, and when the guys came into the house to meet us and see what needed to be moved, they saw a Black family. Their attitudes changed immediately toward us. One mover didn't try to hide his feelings at all.

They took a couple of boxes to the truck, came back, and said, "We are not moving this stuff; your boxes have roaches in them." "Roaches?" I said. "We do not have roaches, man." "Yes, you do," he said. "My truck has other people's furniture inside, and I do not want my truck infested with roaches."

"Sir, I do not have roaches. The roaches must have already been inside your truck before you came here. How is it that your packers packed my stuff, and they never said anything about roaches at the time? But now you're going to stand here and tell me I have roaches? Or are you calling me and my family roaches?" I said, "You just don't want to move my things because I'm Black." And the funny thing about it was he didn't deny it.

It became a back-and-forth argument. They brought the few boxes back inside the house and drove off. I was pissed. Now what was I going to do? I called my general manager and told him what happened. He called someone in the company to see what could be done.

By the time they got back to us, the moving company had already filed a false report claiming I had roaches and needed to fog and roach-bomb the house before they would return to move my things. This pushed us back. I had to wait another three weeks for them to return. The same two guys came back, said, and did the exact same thing: "You have roaches. We are not moving this stuff." At this point, I said, "Get the F out of my house, you racist motherf*****!"

I decided to get a U-Haul and do it myself. Tavis had to come help me load everything. Once it was done, I left the next day. Saying goodbye to my brother was hard. Driving off and seeing him standing there in the mirror, I was all choked up. I got to New Jersey and started work right away. I kept the U-Haul a few extra days because I needed someone to help me unload into the storage unit. I was working, living in a hotel, and looking for a place to live — all at the same time. It took over a month to find something. It was extremely difficult living in a hotel with two babies and my wife. I found a nice townhouse for rent in New Brunswick, a nice area in New Jersey.

I had made a few friends who were able to help me move both times — from the truck to the storage unit, and from the storage unit to the townhouse. New Brunswick is about 40 minutes south of Newark, where my dad lived. Everything was going okay for a while, but we were not happy. We struggled with the kids, trying to find someone we could trust to watch them. By this time, my wife was working as well, about an hour away. I worked about 30 minutes away, and we had only one car. Our schedules were tight — one of us would arrive home just in time for the other to leave for work.

We mostly saw each other on Sundays. On all the other days, it was hit or miss. As life continued, we found a babysitter my new coworker knew. He arranged for us to meet to see if it was a good fit for both sides. It worked out — or so it seemed. We were dropping the kids off like clockwork every day for almost eight hours a day. A few weeks had passed, and my coworker came to me and said, "Hey B, is everything okay?" I said, "Yes, sir. Everything is everything. Why do you ask?" He said, "The babysitter called me because she has been keeping your kids for almost a month, and you haven't paid her." I was shocked. "What do you mean?" I said. "My wife is paying her; there must be a mistake." He said, "No, man, it's not. The girl said you haven't paid her since she's been watching your kids." I didn't know what to do.

I went home, went straight to my wife, and told her what my coworker said. "Is it true?" My wife assured me she had paid the babysitter and was adamant about it. "I pay her every week," she said. I believed her. I went back to work the next day and said, "Hey man, my wife has been paying the lady." He said, "Then somebody is lying."

At lunchtime, he and I went to the breakroom to call the babysitter. I wanted to hear it from her myself. And from her own mouth, she said to me over the phone that we haven't paid at all—not one penny. And she had my kids that day as well. Again, I went back to my wife because now I was like my coworker—somebody was lying. When she and I got into it, I said, "Let's go to the babysitter's house right now."

I wanted to get to the bottom of this. Typically, my wife would drop the kids off, and I would pick them up. We got into the car, heading to her house. My wife was still insisting she had paid. When we got there, my wife said, "Let me go inside and talk to her. I don't want her to feel like we're ganging up on her. That could be intimidating." I said, "Okay, go ahead and fix this."

To this day, I don't know what was said inside that house, but it seemed to iron itself out. I don't think she paid because other things started to happen between us. I would wake up for work only to find she wasn't home. I would get up around 3 a.m. to report to work at 4:30 a.m. With only one car, this was bad for me as an opening manager. Back then, we had no cell phones, only beepers. I paged and paged and paged her, but she never called me back. Because I had no car and my kids were asleep across the hall, I had to call out or call in late to my manager.

Whenever my wife showed up, I didn't have time to argue with her about her whereabouts — I had to jump in the car and get to work. Of course, that affected my performance at work. Mad as hell, wondering where she had been all night, I struggled throughout the day as best I could, wanting to get home to find out what was going on. The problem was that she didn't have time to argue either — she had to get to work. I would tell her, "Please come home after you get off. I don't want to get into trouble at work showing up late like this," while she was driving off. I would call the store asking for her on some days, and they would say, "She's off today." I knew then she must be seeing someone else, but I couldn't prove it.

CHAPTER 8

One night, I switched shifts with a coworker, trying to keep the peace between us. I didn't want our kids to see or hear us arguing. While I was telling her, "I'm working the later shift today," she began to swing at me, telling me I was lying. She went over to the kitchen and started taking all the dishes out of the cabinet, slamming things to the ground. I mean, glass went everywhere. She was having a fit and went into some sort of rage. I was trying to stop her by holding her hands and just holding her, period.

The police had to be called. When they got there, they saw all the broken glass on the floor. The kids were crying and upset. I explained to the officers what happened, and lo and behold, I was late for the closing shift. Damn it! How was I going to explain this to my manager? I had been late for the opening shift, and now I was late for the closing shift. The police made me come down to the station to fill out a statement.

It took about two hours, and when it was all said and done, I arrived at work three hours late. My head wasn't in the right place, but I pushed myself through. A couple of hours passed, and I got a phone call. Over the walkie-talkie, they called from the office and said, "Hey, B, you have a call on line 101." I picked up the phone. "This is B. Can I help you?" Total silence—not a word—but I heard breathing. I called my wife by name and said, "I know that it is you on the phone listening. And as you can hear, I am here at work like I said."

Then I hung up the phone and went back to work. Another hour or so passed. Over the walkie-talkie: "B, come to the front office. B, come to the front office." When I got there, two different New Brunswick police officers were standing there. My heart dropped. I didn't know what was going on—I was scared. They said, "Are you Baron Daniels?" "Yes, I am," I replied. They said, "We're here to serve you a restraining order." "Restraining order? What do you mean? A restraining order for what?" "Your wife filed a domestic violence report against you, and you cannot go within 20 feet of her and the kids." I said, "I didn't do anything but hold her arms to keep her from breaking all the dishes in the kitchen." "You can explain it to the judge when you go to the hearing," they said. "If you try to make contact, go back to the apartment, or go within 20 feet, you will be arrested on the spot." I was unaware that while I was down at the police station filling out my report, she was at home filling out her report of the events and applying for the restraining order too.

I didn't know what to do—I was mad, upset, embarrassed, and had nowhere to go. She had lied on the report, claiming I hit her and roughed her up. It was a total lie, and she knew she was lying. Here I was at work, with all the employees in the office watching this go down. I had to somehow finish my shift, close the building, and find somewhere to stay for the night. I had no clothes or hygiene products, and she didn't care at all. So, I checked into a motel for the night.

The next morning, the police allowed me—under their supervision—to go into the apartment and grab some things I needed. I wasn't allowed to say anything to her or my kids. It was a grab-and-go. That really sucked. It was the worst feeling I had ever experienced. I bounced from place to place for a few weeks—living with a few coworkers I barely knew and staying at the motel. The hearing couldn't come fast enough for me. Before the hearing, my wife called me at work, asking me to come home before the court date. She contacted me first, apologizing. "I'm sorry," she said. "The kids miss you." She told me the white police officer who came to the apartment that night talked her into filing the report. I was missing my family, so I started sneaking into my apartment at night through the back door, under the radar.

One night, we were upstairs chilling, and there was a knock at the door. Knock, knock, knock. We looked out the window and saw a police car and officers at the door. I panicked. "Oh shit," I said. My wife whispered, "Be quiet." She went downstairs. The officers said, "Is Baron here?" She said, "No, he's not." Then they asked if they could come inside to look and make sure I wasn't there. She said, "No, you can't! I said he wasn't here." They continued, "We just want to make sure you and your kids are not in any danger."

Danger? I went from panicked to pissed. What kind of danger had I posed to my family? What in the hell were they talking about? I know now they just wanted to take my ass to jail. I stayed quiet as a church mouse.

After a few minutes, they left. I waited about 30 minutes and quietly eased out the back sliding door. You see, I parked my car a few buildings over from mine. I ran as fast as I could to my car, jumped in, and hauled ass. How dare they say I was a danger to my family, but I couldn't do a damn thing about it. They had badges, the guns, the handcuffs, the jailhouse, and the state of New Jersey to back them up. If I had gotten caught in my own apartment that night, I would say they wanted me to hear them say that so I would react—

trying to get me to come out from hiding, yelling, and trying to protect my feelings and honor. I went and checked into the motel again until we went to court. I couldn't risk it anymore by taking that chance. For the next few weeks, she and my kids stayed with me at the motel in the next city over. Court day arrived. We stood before the judge and told him the same thing about what happened that night.

My wife told him the truth—that I was holding her hands, trying to stop her from breaking the dishes. And the officer had pressured her to file the restraining order against me. She and I strongly defended the fact that I was not a danger to her and my kids, and for the returning officers to suggest that was not right. The judge, in a roundabout way, said, "Well, the officers encounter dangerous husbands on domestic calls all the time. They are doing their jobs." Then the judge asked, "Ms. Daniels, are you asking the courts to drop the restraining order against Mr. Daniels?" She said yes. Then he asked me a dumbass question: "Mr. Daniels, do you wish to file a restraining order against Mrs. Daniels?" In my mind, I was exploding. What in the world was going on? I had never experienced anything like this. "No, Judge," I replied. He then dismissed all charges, made us pay court costs, and sent us on our way. Although it had been a challenging few months, what a relief it was to go home without the pressure of going to jail. I went home and played with my kids all day long. I mean, we had fun. Things seemed to be somewhat back on track. But back to the foolishness within a month. She stopped showing up after work. I had to call off work because of this or catch a cab to work, leaving my kids home alone with instructions on the dos and don'ts.

This was extremely stressful for me. On top of all that, the one car we had was repossessed by the bank for nonpayment. That morning, I woke up when she was home. I walked outside and didn't see the car. Damn, what's going on now? Where is the car? Of course, I was late for work again. My work performance had really declined — not just as a manager but as an employee, period.

My personal life was a roller coaster. I was at work taking care of personal business during half of my shift, trying to figure out what happened to my car and how to get it back. I got it back the next day. My manager called me to the office and said he couldn't continue to allow me to do this. That I needed to consider stepping down as a manager. Man, what a blow to me. At the time, I wasn't seeing the position I was putting my manager in. He went above and beyond to help me be someone big in the company. The hopes and vision he had for me were going down the toilet. But all I saw in my head was, Man, I moved my family here because you asked me to. And I left my best friend and brother in Boston because of you. I said to him, "It's easy for you to say. You don't have kids, so it's not as easy for me." I got up and walked out of his office, getting ready to leave. All the emotions I had been holding in for quite a while came out. It didn't have anything to do with work.

Walking down the hall, I balled up my fist and hit the wall, BOOM! I mean, my whole fist was inside the wall. It was loud, and I didn't even look back. I hit the wall and kept going to my car. I was so mad at everything except my kids. I got home and tried to explain the position that she put me in by not being home with the car, what my manager had suggested. It was almost like talking to the wall. When I got to work the next day, of course, I got called to the office. He had a counseling notice written up for me, willfully damaging company property. I had no choice but to sign it. I was wrong. He asked, "What were you going to do?" I said, "I'm not stepping down; I'm going to get better starting right now." I apologized for breaking the wall. He could have demoted or fired me right then, but he didn't. He has such a heart for people; he forgave me. I tried to balance home and work as best I could. I also made it my business to spend time with my dad and sister. In doing so, we bonded okay. I didn't really question what happened, but he would tell me to ask him anything. Again, to me, what is done is done. When we talked, he said, "Son, I tell you the truth, I came home from work and y'all were gone." He had tried to find us for some time, but back then, the police didn't look too much for you if you were a black family. He had filed a report anyway. And in the report, he wrote, "I'm looking for my son, Baron Teon Daniels," asking all around town if anyone had seen us. Come to find out, my mom had gotten into trouble with some local drug dealers. He didn't know how bad it was or what she had done. I believe at this point is when she changed my name to Baron Teon Knight.

I believe this is when we jumped on the bus or plane and came to Florida, and she didn't look back. I don't know if my dad made right her wrong with these people, but I believe him. The question still haunts me to this very day: Why didn't she change my brother's last name too? Absolutely no contact with my dad for over 20 years. What could she have done? What did my dad do to deserve that? He or anyone was destined not to find me or us at all. They were looking for Baron Teon Daniels. Where did she get "Knight" from? Between missing Tavis, Florida, and home life, things weren't getting any better. I took my manager's advice to step down from management, hoping it would give me more family life.

My pride got into the mix as well at work. What are people going to think now that I'm not a manager? I felt embarrassed; I couldn't look people in the eyes now because I used to be the boss, and now I'm not. My wife continued to do her own thing.

CHAPTER 9

I decided to move back to Florida. I felt going back to where I'm from, around more family members to help with my kids and getting my marriage back on track, would be better. I called my old manager in Florida, asking him if I could come back to work at his location. He said, "No, sir. I don't have any room on my payroll for another full-time employee." I then called the manager that I first met at Wendy's, the one who got me the job at Costco, but by now, she was a general manager of her own location. I told her about my situation and what I was looking forward to coming back to Florida. She said, "Baron, all I have is a night forklift driving position. From 2 p.m. until 10 p.m., Monday through Friday." I said, "I'll take it." She asked me when I could start. It took me a couple of months to get things in position. I sent my family down first; they had to live with relatives. I couldn't come yet until a few weeks later.

I wanted to spend a little more time with my dad and sister. I said my goodbyes to all the employees and the general manager. I said goodbye to my dad, and my sister started crying, which made me cry. But I had to go. I took two days to drive down alone on the road, sightseeing and taking time for myself. I had a few thousand dollars in the bank, just enough to put down on a place to rent. I made it to Florida, moved in with my wife's cousin, and started work right away. This gave me flashbacks — living with someone in their house.

Getting off work at 10 p.m. at night and walking in the door almost at 11 p.m. They gave us a room and tried to make us feel right at home, but this wasn't working for me. I hated it with a passion. I walked on eggshells all the time. You just can't do the things you would do in your own place while living in someone else's. Once I got in, I quickly took a shower and went to bed. Once I got up, we would leave for the day, looking for a place to rent or going over to my wife's parents' house. We didn't want to sit over there like that. We lived there for a month; we found a house for rent. A nice two-bedroom, one-bath house. It had a big family room and a front and back yard. We jumped on it right away; it couldn't come fast enough. My wife and I decided she would not work for a while. She would stay home with the kids so we wouldn't be juggling babysitters. I was working in the Costco warehouse and had to learn how things worked there vs. the depot. It was very different, having members walking all around you while you're trying to work, asking questions that I didn't know the answer to at first, but I held it down like I knew, lol.

The members had no idea I didn't know what I was talking about. I learned a lot and saw the other side of Costco; it was fun. I soon became tired of the night forklift driver position. It felt like all that I had achieved went out the window. I could do more; I could be more with the company. I did something that was unheard of, according to other employees. I asked to work at the front end; this is where the members would check out. The employees called me crazy, saying that I had one of the best jobs in the building. "Why do you want that? No one wants to work there." I said, "I don't mind it at all. I'm a people person, and I love to help and build relationships with people." "You're going to lose your set schedule," they said. "You're going to hate it. You'll see once they put you up there."

I did the exact opposite; I loved it, ringing up members and all. I didn't expect to handle that much money in one order—it was crazy. Some members had two- and three-thousand-dollar orders. That was too much for me to count, so I had to call over my supervisor or the front-end manager to count that. I was fast on the register and had good relationships with the members. Some members only wanted to come through my line, no matter how long the lines were. The managers voted me employee of the month, citing my great attendance, good attitude, a smile on my face, and my register being right on point with the money at the end of my shift. Time went on, and the owner of the house wanted to move back in. We had to move again. Because of the short notice, I took a place that wasn't up to my standards. I didn't want to live with anyone at all.

The location sucked. It was close to the airport, and you could hear planes flying overhead all day and all night. I had to take it, but this time, my wife was working and had her own car too. I made the best of the circumstances, but to me, the place really sucked. I was never a big churchgoer, and my wife's dad was a pastor. For a while, my wife would come home from work and say, "I'm going to go to church," and at first, I didn't think anything of it. "Okay, baby, I'll see you when you get back," I would say. But then I noticed it became more frequent—two and three times a week. And she never wanted to take the kids.

My common sense kicked in; it couldn't be that much church going on every week, coming in at 11 o'clock or 12 o'clock at night. Sometimes the landline phone would ring, and whoever it was would hang up when I said hello. One day, I decided to go up to her job to see her. I walked in and asked for her by name. I was told that she was at lunch and went to the bank down the street. I got back into my car to go find her. I drove down the street and came to the red light to turn right. As I'm looking, waiting for the light to turn green, I see her car at the red light, waiting to turn left. The problem with this is that her car had limo tint—you couldn't see inside that car at all—and the A/C in her car wasn't working. The windows were up, and we live in Florida. It must have been about 97 degrees that day. Why are her windows up? Her light turned green, and she punched it. I mean, she hauled ass. You would have thought she was in the Indy 500. For me to catch up to her, I had to turn right, then go down and make a U-turn. Lord knows I tried to catch up to her.

By the time I did all of that, she was back at work and inside the building, working. I walked up to her and said, "Hi, didn't you see me at the light?" She said no. I asked, "Why were your windows up in this Florida heat? Who did you have in the car?" "No one," she said. "I was down the street from my job. I just let them up early, that's all. I didn't want to make a scene at my job." But I knew she was lying to me, straight to my face. I said, "I came here to have lunch with you. That's why I came, but you've already had lunch, so I'll see you later." I couldn't prove anything, so I let it be and went on living. As her AC stopped working, other problems started with her car. We went back to one car. I was working full-time and in school, trying to get my high school diploma.

The day came when we were both off from work. She said, "I'm going to church tonight." I said, "No, you're not. We're going to spend time as a family with the girls." She said, "But I want to go to church." "Okay, we're all going to go then," I said. She quickly changed her mind. "Okay, we will hang out. It will be a movie night," she said. I ran to our local movie rental store and rented a few movies for us. When I got back home, she was dressed to leave. "Why are you dressed?" I said. She replied, "I'm leaving and going to church." But this time, she said it more with an attitude and argument. "No, you're not!" I said. "Yes, I am," she said. This was going on in front of my girls. I didn't want them to see all this again. I was afraid she would start breaking things again and, moreover, call the police and file another restraining order on me. So, I backed off for the sake of avoiding an argument and to keep the peace, and she went. The girls and I watched a few movies until we all fell asleep.

A few days later, I headed off to work earlier than usual. You see, I was also enrolled in school and had an exam coming up. It was hard trying to balance work, home, and study time. I would get to work sometimes an hour and a half early and sit in my car to study.

Then, I went to clock in when it was time and came back to study in the car during lunchtime.

This particular day before work, I was sitting in the car and needed something to write with. I reached for my pen but dropped it between the seat and console. Trying to grab it with my fingers, my hand wouldn't fit, so I had to reach behind the seat to get it. In doing so, feeling around underneath the seat, I felt a piece of cloth or clothing of some sort.

When I pulled it out, it was a part of my wife's lingerie. "What the hell! How in the world did this get there?" I was now totally convinced she was fooling around with another man. I called her immediately. When she answered the phone, I got straight to the point. "I found your lingerie underneath the seat of the car. How did it get there?" She went on to say it must have been one of the girls. "You know how they go through my stuff, playing around." I said, "No, they didn't do that. And if so, why would they place it under the seat? Furthermore, all your late-night church-going is starting to make sense now." I wasn't getting anywhere over the phone. I went into my work and went to the manager and said, "I can't work today. I just found out my wife is having an affair, and I need to go home." The manager was totally understanding and gave me permission to leave.

When I got home, I didn't care if she called the police or anything. I was tired of her shit. I mean, I went in on her — nothing physical, all verbal. I said, "I know you're sleeping with someone. Stop denying it. You can cry tears until you fill the bathtub. You are a liar and a cheat. I knew you were cheating back then, but I had no proof, and I convinced myself not to listen to my instincts. I have the proof now, and you know it. Who is he?" I asked. She denied it for hours, crying all in front of our girls, but still blaming it on one of them. That told me right then, people will put the blame on anyone other than themselves. Around 8:00 that night, she finally came clean.

This is where she went into her acting role — crying uncontrollably, reaching out to hug me, squeezing me tight, not letting me go. "I'm sorry, I'm sorry," she said. She came clean, telling me how it all started, how that's who she had in the car the day I came to her job for lunch and the windows were up. The damage was done. The shit hurt, but I became numb to the pain. You're sleeping with your coworker, someone you will see tomorrow and the next day and the next day after that. How am I supposed to handle that? I didn't want to lose my kids or separate from them. I had to go see a therapist for a while. Then we went together. All that the therapist said was okay, I guess. What kept me in check and stopped me from doing something stupid and getting prison time was my girls. Believe me, it crossed my mind all the time, and for a long time after. I had to force myself not to think about it and move on. In doing so, I found myself looking for a girlfriend on the side. Hell, if she can have an affair, so can I. I wanted revenge, payback. I wanted her to feel my pain. Nevertheless, we continued to work it out—that's all I could do. We moved again, but this time into a nice townhouse. Man, did I really like this place.

CHAPTER 10

By this time, I was back at the depot loading trucks for my old manager. My oldest was starting 1st grade, and my wife had quit the job. Things seemed good for a while, hanging out with the family. But she soon became tired of the housewife thing. She wanted to be able to get out of the house. She took a job at the video store and then became the manager.

Not long after that, the same old person came back, amplified. Because the video store stayed open until 11 p.m., she worked late. On most nights, I was asleep by the time she got home. Little by little, again, I would wake up for work and she wouldn't be home. I called, I called, I called her cell phone with no answer. So, I would have to call out of work because I had no car and no one home to watch my kids. Or she would roll in with just enough time for me to jump into the car and haul ass to work. I was either late or called out of work all the time. I knew she was having another affair, but again, I ignored my instincts. I found myself having to disconnect the battery or the starter of the car. She got bolder and wouldn't come home at all. I would have to take my kids over to the in-laws so I could report to work. It got to the point that she didn't even care about our kids or me losing my job. It was all about her. She started not coming home for days.

Come to find out, she and her sister, her sister's boyfriend, and her boyfriend all moved into their own apartment. I was done. I had to figure out something — what to do about my kids. I needed help with them so I could work. She didn't want them or try to help me with them. So, I decided to let my in-laws keep them until the weekend, then I would pick them up on Fridays. Just until I got things situated for the three of us. I was arranging daycare and aftercare, asking female family members if they could help me with getting their hair done regularly, getting school prepared, etc. Boy, but they had another plan I didn't see coming. All of them — the in-laws, dad, mom, sister, and both brothers.

I'm sitting home on a Saturday morning, and I hear a knock on the door. Knock, knock, knock! I look through the peephole and see a police officer standing there. I opened the door; it's the Greenacres Police Department. I thought, what is going on? What happened? Who's dead? They asked, "Are you Baron Daniels?" "Yes, I am. What's going on?" They said, "We have a restraining order for you." "On me? For what? By whom?" The order was filed by your wife for sexual abuse of your daughter. That you cannot come within 100 feet of your wife and kids or return to this residence. This residence? My wife moved out three months ago, I said. She doesn't live here. "On the contrary, sir. She's right over there."

When I looked to my right, my wife was sitting in her car along with her boyfriend, watching all this go down. They were smiling and laughing. You see, they had gotten evicted from the apartment they were renting for nonpayment of rent. Her backup plan was to go down to the courthouse and file a false report. Like before, she knew this would go in her favor.

I had no idea she could be so evil, but it got worse. The police officers said, either I leave or go to jail. They allowed me to gather a few things, mostly my clothing and my dog. I was loading my car, and my wife and boyfriend continued to watch and smile. They were cocky as could be because the cops were on standby to keep the peace.

My emotions were running high; I didn't know what to do or where to go. As I got into my car to leave, they got out of her car and walked into my house. After all the work I'd done — getting ready for my kids, babysitters, daycare, and aftercare in place — it was all taken away. I drove off, and the only place I could go was the one place I didn't want to: my mom's apartment. Of course, she welcomed me in. That's because she was four months behind on her rent. I had to give her $600 right off the cuff. Emotionally, I was a mess; all my feelings went out the door. I lost my wife, kids, and place all together. After paying a month's rent for my mom, I had a few hundred dollars left. I had my job, thank God. I continued to work. I didn't care anymore about anyone; I started seeing another woman and moved in with her into her apartment.

Well, I went back and forth between Mom and her. A whole year went by without any contact with my kids. It wasn't until I met my new girlfriend, Quovadis—she's the one!—that things started to change. My car had been repossessed by the bank. Quovadis took her income tax check, took me down, and got me a new car. I'm talking brand new, hot off the press new. She got me to start thinking about my kids and got the ball rolling to go see them. She knew that I didn't read the restraining order all the way through. I didn't know where my kids lived, but I knew where their granddad pastored a church. So, I waited until Sunday and drove down to Boca Raton. I called the Boca Police Department and had them run my name in the system just to make sure I was clear of the order. They came back and said, "Yes, sir. That order expired a year ago." So, I drove over to the church and waited outside until it let out. I was parked right up front, watching people come out and leave. Some stood around talking for a few minutes. I didn't see my kids at all. I almost drove off, but suddenly, my wife walked out. She didn't see me sitting in the car because she had never seen that car before.

The next thing I saw was Tiffany, my oldest, coming out first, right behind her, Dominique, the youngest. I jumped out of the car and said, "Tiffany! Dominique!" When they looked and saw me standing, they both screamed and said, "Daddy! Daddy!" running in my direction, screaming and crying. They both jumped into my arms, one on each side. Oh man, what a feeling it was, seeing my kids after a year. Tears and snot of joy that day. My shirt was wet as hell. I didn't pay any attention to anyone else in the parking lot. They were all looking at us, but I didn't care. My wife walked over to me and said, "My dad wants you to come inside. He wants to talk to you." Before I knew it, I said, "Fuck you, and fuck him. I don't want to talk to him or you. I'm here for my kids." They were scared I was going to make a scene in front of his congregation. But I was cool and didn't make a scene; I continued talking to and hugging my girls. I told them, "Daddy is sorry for being away so long. I'm going to get you as soon as I can."

I left that day and felt a recharge in my body to get my kids. By this time, Quovadis and I were living together and wanted to get married. I filed for divorce from my then-wife and filed for full custody of my kids. But let me tell you, it got worse for me in the months to come. I was trying to keep it simple, but she and her parents came out with all guns blazing.

In her divorce filing (my then wife) her and her parent said that I sexually assaulted my daughter. Touching her in her private places on her body. My wife wrote, her mom (my mother-in-law) called her and said. She noticed my daughter looking strange one day and she said to my daughter, what's wrong? Has your daddy been touching you? That my daughter said yes. Where has your dad touched you? When we go to the pool, he would hold me by my legs or butt. This is a community pool where people are all around, kids running and playing. Because she wrote that, the restraining order was on again. I was furious, this is the same person that I use to sleep in the same bed with.

This was terrible. I had to endure her and her boyfriend kicking me out of my apartment, not seeing my kids for a year, three restraining orders within three years, and now I'm being accused of sexual assault. We had a court hearing scheduled 90 days out. The day came, and my mom went to the hearing with me. My wife showed up with her dad, mom, and boyfriend. Her dad was dressed in his clergy church uniform. To show the courts that he and his family are in the ministry, that they are people of God, they lied through the whole hearing. They were so self-righteous. Of course, she was awarded the kids, and they found a reason to put me on supervised visitation, but not enough to press charges. I had to endure the courts questioning me all about my relationship with my girls. It felt like a million questions.

For a year, every other weekend, I had to go to the courthouse to see my kids. They had a play set up in the back for all the parents who had to be supervised. I hated it. I had to check in and be patted up and down by an officer. Then, I had to wait for my kids to show up. We sat at a table with a person monitoring every move I made. Every word spoken was written down. I could only hug them for a few minutes, then, most of the time, I could not touch them. It was 4 hours every other Saturday. We just played games or talked or watched TV. It sucked. We were not allowed to leave together; they would leave first, and I had to wait 30 minutes after. I was ordered to pay child support, pay for all insurance, and cover the in-between stuff. This supervised visitation went on for a year.

Once the courts were convinced I wasn't a sexual predator, they sent someone to my apartment to evaluate my living conditions. By this time, Q and I were married. We didn't have much. No furniture or nicer things. With the amount of money going out and just enough coming in, it was extremely tight. The social worker had to walk all through the apartment looking around and wrote, "The furniture is worn out, the TV is sitting on top of boxes, and his new wife has two boys." But the courts finally gave me unsupervised visitations.

Even then, I was very careful how I hugged and touched my kids. From that point on, day by day, all I did was work. Seven days a week, twelve to fifteen hours a day. Taking care of my new and old family without complaining. Q was very supportive throughout my rough patches. When the girls came over, she stepped up to the plate while I was either at work or sleeping. She had games or activities for them all. We did the best we could with what we had. A few times, we didn't pay our rent just so we could go do something with the kids. At some point, Q and I started to go to a church where a pastor was teaching the congregation about finances and credit. He taught what it took to buy a home, getting your credit right, and programs out there for first-time buyers.

We took hold of that and put a plan in action for our credit. It made total sense; he brought scriptures to back up his teachings — trusting in God and having faith. Pay your bills, pay your bills on time, and pay who you owe. And that's what we did. For two years, we worked on our credit and saved money to buy a house. We were totally new to this; we've always rented. It was hard work, getting in contact with the creditors, making payment arrangements, or settling the account. If we owed them $2,000 and the account was five years old, we would offer $1,000 to settle the account. Sometimes it worked; other times, they wanted the full amount of what's owed.

This is where payment arrangements came into play. But we started with the smallest amount first and went to the most owed. We took one account at a time. I continued working two jobs, taking care of my responsibilities. Costco was growing fast; my family was growing up fast. I wanted to be the best dad and husband I could be. My mistake in my last marriage was not coming to the new. Q and I just wanted to get married. I didn't even ask her; I just said, "We're getting married." Lol. We filed for our license, and the state of Florida sent us to a marriage program for two weeks. The divorce rate was high, I guess. They wanted to make sure we understood what we were doing. The program was fun. We met other couples getting married, too.

One thing I learned was that too many people put all their money and time into planning for the wedding and not the longevity of the marriage. We completed our two weeks and scheduled the ceremony at the courthouse. We had a few friends and a few close family members, and we did it. It was short and sweet, then we went on a small weekend getaway to Orlando. When we got back, it was back to the grind. We both worked, trying to reach our goal. I would still get my girls every other weekend. We could only afford a two-bedroom apartment, so the boys would sleep in the living room when they came over. They happily gave up their room to the girls. It was funny watching them bicker back and forth when it came to cleaning around the house.

The girls, for some strange reason, thought they had maids and butlers. They felt that because they were only here for a few days, they shouldn't have to clean the kitchen or their bedroom. I nipped that in the bud right out of the gate. I explained to them how it was going to be when they came over. I had all four of them in the living room and laid down the law of the land. We are a blended family, and we must work together. It wasn't easy, but I didn't waver. I meant what I said and said what I meant. Little by little, it got better and better. I still had to keep the peace between the girls' moms. She would try to make me react to her foolishness. I had moved on from her, and my love for her had turned into hatred. By then, she had already been with three to four men. I would go to the church where her dad was pastoring to see my girls sing a song or do a recital. If she and her parents knew I was coming, they would have the boyfriend stand up and read aloud a love poem to her. Or he would bring a dozen roses so the whole church and I could see.

Trying to make me jealous with the extra holding of hands or kisses. The dad would make some sort of announcement from the pulpit about his future son-in-law. They would go through all this before my girls would do what I came to see them do. I didn't fret or waver because I knew it was a show, and not from the heart. This is what most of the people who call themselves Christians do. The drama, wanting people to think they are so holy and in touch with the Lord, when they are not even close. The mom would be smiling and clapping her hands with tears of joy, sitting in the first ladies' row of the church. She made sure I saw her standing up, giving a standing ovation when the new boyfriend walked down the aisle with the roses.

I'd be lying if I said it didn't bother me. I felt some type of way, but they didn't know it. I think the more they did things like that, the stronger I became. I think I even stood up a time or two and gave a standing ovation myself, lol. Because I knew who they were — the real deal, holy field. How evil they can be. I mean, think about it: the things they said about me to the courts in our divorce just to get custody of my kids. Things that could send someone to prison for a long time. They did it and didn't think twice about it. And yet they call themselves godly people. I endured all that. Maybe this was my punishment for the things I had done.

It was a long road ahead; in my darkest days, I never said anything negative to my kids about their mom. They were too young to understand. It made my marriage stronger with Q. She really had my back. There were times, after paying the bills and the creditors we owed, that we had no money at all. We had food in the house and gas in the cars. It was so bad. One time, Q and I had gotten some free tickets to the yearly outdoor festival. Earth, Wind & Fire was there the day we went. They were performing later in the evening.

We got there around 11 a.m. There were food and beer vendors all over the festival. After walking around for about 30 minutes, we got thirsty. I couldn't even buy Q a bottle of water. It was bad. We were there until 9 p.m. that night and didn't have any money to buy anything. Thirsty and embarrassed, I saw a few friends out there but was too ashamed to ask to borrow some money. We were miserable, hot, hungry, and thirsty, out there for 10 hours. After that, I made a promise to myself that I'd never do that again. I'd never go to any other events of any kind without money in my pocket. We got home and attacked the refrigerator. We finally paid off all the debt we had after a two-year run.

We started putting money away and stopped living paycheck to paycheck. It wasn't much, but it was more than we had in the past. Heading in the right direction, we were even able to take a couple of weekend cruises. Something I had never done. Q was the one, always planning things for us and the kids to do. Once the credit score and the money were right, the pastor of our church hooked us up with a realtor. We started looking for a place to buy. We must have seen 15 condos. We found a condo that Q fell in love with. It was beautiful. It was the one for us. The seller and her realtor were there when we went to see the place. She saw how excited Q was about the place. The seller even offered to throw in the furniture that was there. It was listed for sale at one hundred and ninety-five thousand dollars.

We told our realtor to make an offer for one hundred and ninety-three thousand dollars, with the seller paying the closing costs. The next day, my realtor called us. "Congratulations," she said. The seller agreed to the offer. We were as happy as we could be. A few hours later, my realtor called us back with bad news. She said the seller's realtor had called her and said the seller had changed her mind. She now wanted one hundred and ninety-five thousand dollars. You see, they thought the excitement Q and I had for the place was going to make us make a bad decision. When my realtor told us that, I said absolutely not. We will not do any such thing. She agreed to the offer, and now she's gotten greedy. I told my realtor to tell her realtor this: her place had been for sale for over two months. She just killed the deal for us because she wasn't a person of her word. I wouldn't buy it now if she came with a counteroffer for one hundred and ninety-two thousand dollars. I didn't like that at all, and we walked away. The very next condo we saw was bigger, and the price was right for our budget.

The seller did what he said he would, and we bought it. The whole experience was great. I'm sure the seller who changed her mind about the price that made us walk away was kicking herself in the ass. We saw her driving by my unit often, but nevertheless, it wasn't meant to be. Once we got settled in, I decided to go see my dad and sister. Going back was good for my soul. Going back a little older, a little wiser, making peace with Dad. I didn't want him to feel bad about the past. But that was easier said than done.

For a while, it was like Dad was trying to buy me everything or put money in my pocket every chance he had — almost trying to buy my love. But all I wanted was just to get to know more about him. What was his background? Are my grandparents alive, and where? Did he have any siblings? You see, I didn't ask these kinds of questions before. I learned my grandparents were dead, and he had no siblings. Dad worked in some sort of factory back in the day and owned a nightclub. He had gotten hurt. A small piece of metal got into his eye. From what I'm told, they tried to save it for a while, but he was in so much pain, and the vision was 90% gone. The doctors had to take the eye out. Dad said he was blind now, but the pain was gone. He felt so much better.

It took a few years for his one eye to get strong enough until he couldn't tell he had one eye, unless he looked into a mirror to put in his prosthetic eye. He couldn't tell. He was able to drive and all. Sometimes the prosthetic eyeball would be out of place, and I'd say, "Hey, Dad, fix your eye, man," lol. He also was a loan shark. He had a mean side too. I'd ride with him and watch him loan money out and pick money up, plus the interest that was owed to him. And good god, if the person didn't have his money, he wasn't physically violent, but he would curse out the person something bad about his money. This big 6-foot-1-inch, dark-skinned, 220-pound man was my pops. I would go back often, even building a great relationship with my stepmom. She was a down-to-earth person and made me feel like I was her son.

Every time I'd come back to Newark, she'd cook this big breakfast every morning and this big dinner every night. From scratch, too; I felt like a king. They went above and beyond making sure I was welcomed. My sister was very smart, a straight-A student. My stepmom didn't play when it came to education. She was very strict with her; she was reading at a 10th-grade level in elementary school. Reading better than I could, she had chores around the house as well. I mean, my stepmom had a schedule. But all in all, we bonded over the years. My stepmom and dad would eventually separate.

Even with the separation, I would still go back and spend time with both. In fact, I spent more time with my stepmom than my dad. He had too much going on and a lifestyle I wasn't comfortable with. I would fly in and stay with my stepmom and go visit my dad, or he would come over and hang out with us. He and I would ride out, but I would say, "Hey, dad, if we're picking up money, I'll stay here."

I made the best of it. Q and I continued to grow. We had hard times here and there. We had fun, too; we'd traveled to different parts of Florida. That was all Quovadis. She was the one broadening my eyes. Most of my vacations were staycations. I have never been to any big theme park or Key West. She was on it; since we've been together, I've been to Key West, St. Augustine, New York, and all the Caribbean Islands many times. And I asked myself, "Why me? I don't understand. I've listened to many preachers over the years. I thought they knew what they were talking about when they were teaching, that God was giving them the knowledge, up in the pulpit or on stage preaching, getting the congregation all pumped up. Some would teach, 'Pay your tithe; if you want God to bless you, you must pay your tithe. Show God you trust Him with your money. It's not your money anyway.' I've seen some preachers say, 'God is telling me right now. There are 50 people in here now that should give $1,000 right now. If you want Him to bless you, get up out of your seats, you know who you are.' And the people would jump up and run to the front of the church and throw money or checks on the stage because he gave a two-hour sermon on giving and tithing. 'If you want God to heal your body and bless you with more money than you could handle, show God you trust Him first, and He will heal and bless you.' The stage would be full of money. Then the preacher would say, 'God is now telling me there are 25 people in here right now that need to give $500. You may not be able to give $1,000, but you could give $500. If you want God to heal and bless you, get up out of your seats and give $500.' And just like the $1,000 crew..." The people jumped up, running to the stage and throwing money or checks onto the stage. The stage would be covered with money. They had to have someone pick up the money as the people brought it. Then he would say, "God is telling me there are 10 people in here that need to give 250 dollars," and again, they would jump up and bring the money up to the stage. Whoever was left, he said, "Bring what you can; God is only going to heal and bless you based on how much you give." This went on for a while. It just didn't make any sense to me. I gave what I could because I didn't know any better. Almost every church service involved money or giving in some sort of fashion.

I was up late one night watching TV; it must have been around 3 a.m. I was watching one of the Christian channels, and the preacher said to the TV watchers and the congregation, "Next Sunday, we are going to have a burning bill and debt cancellation service. Bring all your bills next week and bring them up to your television if you're watching from home. God is going to cancel all your bills and wipe out all your debt." That was kind of where I drew the line in the sand. But I tuned in just to watch what happened. The following week, the preacher had the stage set up with some sort of big metal barrels and the fire department standing by. There were hundreds of people there. The preacher said to them all, "Bring all your bills up to the stage and throw them inside the barrel." It was well-organized, starting with the front row, and row by row, I watched hundreds of people come up to the stage with stacks of papers in hand and throw them inside the barrels. Once everyone brought their bills up, he said, "Now each of you get a love offering ready, starting at 100 dollars, and give." And like clockwork, the money was flowing. After that, he set the barrels on fire. He said, "Your bills are now burned and canceled; God has done a miracle for you." And these people screamed, cheered, and clapped, thinking that God had taken away all their bills. The preacher turned to the TV watchers and said, "Bring your bills up to the TV, along with a love offering (money) of any amount. Send it to the address on the bottom of your TV screen. Once you've done that, take your bills and tear them in half. God has done a miracle for you; no more bills."

So, I took one bill up to the TV, sent a small love offering, and tore the bill up and threw it in the trash. Guess what happened? About 30 days later, I got another bill—the same bill, with a late fee. Lol. I was tickled at this; I knew better but did it anyway. I knew, since I got re-billed again, all those hundreds of people did too. This is when I started to open my Bible a little more because the preacher hardly did, and if they did, they would read a small part—four or five verses—and talk for 2 hours. Prosperity all the time, making people think you had to buy your way into heaven. "God has nothing for you if you don't trust Him and give."

Another time, I wanted to see how much this particular church wanted to save my soul. They would be on the popular Christian channel all the time. They would be on a roll, talking about how magnificent God is, how He's all-powerful, all-mighty, and wonderful. They would get the people all motivated, clapping, hollering, and praising the Lord. At the end of the show—yes, the show I mentioned — the church made an announcement for those at home watching on TV. The announcement, with a voice in the background, said, "Do you want God to bless you? Do you want God to heal your body? Order this gold-painted plaque with Isaiah 41:10 engraved. The scripture reads: Do not fear, for I am with you; do not be dismayed, for I am your God. I will strengthen you and help you; I will uphold you with my righteous right hand. Call this number now, and we'll send you this life-changing plaque for a small love offering starting at $60." So, I called the number, and they sent me the enclosed envelope with the return information, along with other items you could purchase.

I wrote a small letter asking if they could send me the plaque with the scriptures. This would really help me and change my life, getting me on track with the Lord. I mailed it back without a love offering. I waited for about three weeks because this church was in Texas. Another letter came from them with the same information as the first one. So, I wrote another letter, asking again if they could send me the plaque. This would help me. Only this time, I added, "I can't afford to send any love offering. Money is tight for me right now, but I'd sure love for God to bless me," and I mailed it back and waited. I waited and waited and waited until I called them after a few months had passed. When I got them on the phone at the church office, I said, "Hi, my name is Baron, and I saw your church service on TV a few months back. I saw that you all were wanting the Lord to bless me with a plaque with Isaiah 41:10. I called your number, and your organization sent me the information twice. I couldn't send a love offering because times are tough for me right now, and I explained that in my return letter to your organization. I haven't heard anything back from your organization concerning my walk with the Lord. Can you help me?" I asked. The lady replied, "You didn't send a love offering?" I said, "No, ma'am." She said, "Well, we're not able to send you the plaque without a love offering." I said, "Don't you all care about my blessings?" It became a back-and-forth with them. I didn't want the plaque, but I wanted to prove a point: most churches today don't care anything about a person's soul. It's all about the money and nothing else. I guess they said, "To hell with you if you can't send us money." I still see the same church on TV all the time, ranting and raving about the same old thing. For a while after that, I didn't give God much attention.

I continued to live and work. I felt all the churches were the same when I finally made the decision to go to church and join. I became a volunteer, helping in the media department—setting up the microphones and running the soundboard, recording the services a couple of Sundays for a few hours out of the month. But then it became every Sunday, for 5 to 6 hours every Sunday. This became a part-time job because the church had moved to a location where the volunteers had to set up the stage, run wiring, and pull things out of the storage room to set up before service time. I had to get there at 8 a.m., and service started at 10 a.m., so it was work. Plus, the pastor had a meeting with all department heads every Sunday for 30 to 40 minutes. Service would end around 1 p.m. Then we had to put everything back into the storage room and break down all we had set up.

I did it for a while; it was fun, and I thought it was for the Lord. Then the church started having the volunteers fill out a request form if you wanted a Sunday off. The form had two checkboxes: one for "approved" and the other for "denied." The department head had a meeting with us telling us this. I said, "Hold up, wait a minute, pump the brakes. I'm not filling out some request form asking for permission not to volunteer! What sense does that make? We are volunteering, not getting paid." He explained, "It's just so we can be prepared and make plans if someone won't be here." I said, "Okay, then the request form needs to be redone. It should be more like, 'Please give us the dates you will not be able to volunteer,' not with checkboxes for approval or denial." I didn't want to be that guy, but dang, that rubbed me the wrong way. And there were more and more little things that didn't sit right with me. So, I decided to leave. I learned a lot from the pastor, but it was time to go; there had to be more to what I'd seen from church. All that was being taught about tithing and giving or you will not be blessed by God didn't match up to my life at all.

I started to rethink all that I'd been through thus far. I was blessed and had more than enough to survive. I had a roof over my head, food in the refrigerator, and a few dollars in the bank. What are they talking about except the same thing: be a giver? But something hit me in the inner core of my body. I believed God was talking to me. "Baron, be a giver," He said, "and it doesn't have to be money. It could be you spending time with someone and being a listening ear, or helping someone in a time of need, whatever that may be. Give advice, give them My word, or buy someone something to eat." That was right on the money. If someone on the street would ask me for money, I was very selective about who I gave money to. It was very rare that I gave money out, but if someone asked me for something to eat, I was—and still am—on it. I'll feed anyone who asks or, if I saw a homeless person, I would offer. I want to get my life in order with God's plans for me. I still was doing things I shouldn't have; I struggled with xxx videos, especially since they are so easy to get to online. Back in the day, you had to go to the

XXX video store and rent them. I remember parking in the back and walking through the front door with my hat on, hoping no one I knew saw me walk in.

But now it's just a click of the mouse. I was surfing the web one day and came across a pastor who was teaching from the Bible. He told the congregation and the TV watchers to open their Bibles and follow him. He was talking about false teachers and prophets, that many people are going to hell because of them. He said, a pastor's job is to prepare you to meet God. He said, "Get yourselves right with God, get out of these false churches that are always talking about giving and prosperity. Get away from those kinds of churches. They're not teaching you to repent! Stop sinning, ask God to forgive you for your wrongdoing." He said, "Do you want to spend all eternity in hell?" You need to repent while you still have a chance. Tomorrow is not promised to you or me. He said these so-called pastors are teaching you, "Once saved, always saved," but that is a lie. I've heard that so many times, that once I get saved, I can't go to hell. I can live however I want to because I'm saved. It just didn't make any sense. He said, "Open your Bible to 2nd Chronicles, chapter 15, verse 1," and it says, "And the Spirit of God came upon Azariah the son of Oded; and he went out to meet Asa, and said to him, 'Hear me, Asa, and all Judah and Benjamin: The Lord is with you, while you be with Him; and if you seek Him, He will be found of you; but if you forsake Him, He will forsake you.'" I wanted the definition for "forsake." Forsake means to abandon, renounce, or give up something. The dictionary read that to forsake a person is to leave them entirely, usually in a moment of need. That's plain and simple.

Now I thought to myself, what else am I being taught wrong? I started to pay more attention to this minister. He was talking about things I hadn't heard any other minister teach at all. And the most important thing: he asked everyone in the congregation and the TV watchers to open their Bibles and see it and read it for themselves. He said, "Don't take my word for it, read it. It's in the Bible that you are carrying." He gave the book, chapter, and verse every time. He talked about how Christmas isn't Jesus' birthday. Surely everyone knows Jesus was born on December 25th, RIGHT? Well, dig this: once a woman gets pregnant, she carries for nine months if everything goes smoothly. Can we agree on that? Now open your Bible to Luke, chapter 1, verse 26. The Bible says: "And in the sixth month the angel Gabriel was sent from God unto a city of Galilee, named Nazareth. To a virgin engaged to a man whose name was Joseph, of the house of David; and the virgin's name was Mary. And the angel came in unto her, and said, Hail, thou that art highly favored by God, blessed are you among women. And when she saw him, she was troubled at what he was saying and cast in her mind what manner of salutation this should be. And the angel said unto her, fear not, Mary: for you have found favor with God. And behold, you shall conceive in your womb and bring forth a son, and shall call his name Jesus." Now, I'm counting in my head: the sixth month is June. Nine months from June is March or April of the following year, depending on the day in June she got pregnant. But for sure, it isn't December, so where did this come from? Whence came this deviation is what I want to know. I could go on with more of this bad teaching, but I'm learning to be very, very cautious with who I'm listening to.

As I'm getting older, I start thinking more about death and the soul. I know people and classmates who have already died, either by violence or disease. The ones who were violent were inevitable because of their lifestyles, the things they were doing. I had one classmate who fought all the time. He was ready to get it on with anybody, anywhere. He was good at fighting and won just about all his fights, so his confidence was at 100. I remember us in elementary school when someone sucker-punched him in the eye. I mean, he never saw it coming. He decided to ride home on the same school bus as the kid who punched him. The kid who punched him was sitting in the back of the bus. When we arrived at the bus stop, he got off first and stood next to the door, waiting for the kid to get off. The kid must have called someone from home to come to the bus stop after school because he got off. He had one hand inside his book bag when the kid who got sucker-punched lunged at him. His hand came out of that book bag with the biggest butcher knife I've ever seen. His hand went back and was coming forward to stab the other kid. But thank goodness there were adults who jumped in between the two and stopped it before it got started. He could have died that day; his ego was hurt bad. He didn't want people to know he got punched in the face, and he couldn't get even with the kid. I think the other kid's parents pulled him out of the school and sent him to another. I would have thought my classmate would have calmed down from wanting to fight so much, but he didn't. Years later, in high school, it must have been a weekend. Back then, most Black families didn't have a washer and dryer at home; we had to go to the laundromat. He was at the laundromat and got into it with another patriot. He beat the guy up good and was proud of it too.

The guy said to him, "I'll be right back." Instead of using common sense and leaving or apologizing to the person, his pride kicked in, and he stayed there waiting for round 2. Well, when the guy showed up and saw my classmate waiting, he walked up to him, pulled a gun out from his waist, and shot him right in the chest. This guy must have had a cannon inside his pants because he blew a hole in my classmate. He died right on the street. He died brave, only nineteen years old. Such a shame. I think the guy who killed him got 5 years in jail. Even if you don't believe in God, you will one day, and hopefully, it isn't too late. I'm thanking God every day that He allows me to live each day I wake up, and it gives me another chance to get right with Him. I could have died so many times, but He spared me.

All these years since I was born, I never spent a night in the hospital. That was until the pandemic. It hit the US, and people were dropping like flies. I personally know people who got COVID and passed away from it. Somehow, I caught it the same day I found out my co-worker had passed away from it that morning. I was sitting at my desk at work when suddenly I got hot. My body temperature jumped up quickly. I drove home and took a cool shower. When my wife came in, I said, "Boo, stay back. I have a fever." I made an appointment to get tested the next day. A few days went by, and it came back positive. Like everyone else, I had to quarantine myself to my room. The fever was coming and going. I stayed in bed for four days. The nighttime was the worst. I started tossing and turning in the bed, then on the floor, just trying to make it comfortable. I couldn't sleep through the night. I wasn't eating, just sipping on water, and not taking the right medicine for the fever. Then it became hard to breathe and catch my breath. I was lying in bed, and it felt like I was running a race. I was panting; something wasn't right. I called Quovadis and said, "Boo, something isn't right. I can't catch my breath. Take me to the hospital." I got to the ER, and they hooked me up to an IV. The doctor came in and said, "I'm thinking about admitting you. Let's see how you respond to the IV and breathing treatment, and we will see."

After a few hours on the right fluids from the IV and breathing treatment, I felt a little better. They sent me home. The next day, around 5 p.m., I started panting again. I called my wife again, "Boo, I can't catch my breath. Take me back to the hospital." I remember sitting in the emergency room; I felt terrible, trying to stay strong, waiting to be called back. I got up and walked over to the vending machine to buy a water bottle. I walked back to my seat and sat down. Looking around the room, the next thing I knew, people were standing over me, picking me up off the ground, putting me on a gurney, and asking me my name, what day of the week it was, and my age. I didn't know what the hell happened at first, but once I came to my senses, I realized I had passed out. My body was on fire, I was weak, and it hurt to breathe. They took me to the back and ran me through some machine that scanned my whole body. They said when I fell, I hit my head on the floor. They wanted to see my brain, but I don't remember hitting anything at all. Once my brain scan came back normal, they found that the fever and lung infections were my problems. It was bad. About midnight, they admitted me and took me up to the COVID floor.

They stripped me down to my underwear and t-shirt and packed ice bags all around my body — under my armpits, between my legs, and behind my head. The IV was put in, and I was on oxygen. The IV stand must have had five bags hanging on it, pumping fluid into me. I had no idea if my wife knew what was going on; I was too sick to call her. I thought, this could be it. Every time they came to check my fever, it was 101 or 102 for two days. My bed was soaked and wet, I was soaked and wet. Then, on the second day, they came in and exchanged the sheets with me in bed. They flipped me over like a pancake. I was still weak but able to call my wife and let her know I was hanging on. On the third day, my fever broke, my body temperature was normal, but I was still hurting. My lungs were hurting, and I was breathing with short breaths. They were pumping so much fluid into me, I was peeing every five minutes. I had a pee bottle hanging on the side of the bed, and I filled it up every 20 minutes. I was calling the nurse to empty it out on the regular. I tried sitting up, but when I did, the room would start spinning. I had to lay my head back down. The nurses came in every two hours, all through the night. I had to get a shot in the stomach for blood clots. On the fourth day, a nurse came in looking at my charts. Her exact words were, "Uh-uh, honey, you need to get out of that bed and get going." She changed my socks, changed my IV bags, and gave me my meds. Her words got me motivated. Because up until then, I was just lying there, almost wasting away. I sat myself up and stayed sitting up no matter what, no matter how much the room was spinning. After a while, I was able to get out of bed and walk to the bathroom to pee instead of using the pee bottle. On days five and six, I was breathing 1000% better. I felt my strength coming back, slowly but surely.

On day seven, the doctor came in and said, "You're getting discharged today, you are going home." I was ready — weak, but ready. I called my wife, "Boo, I'm coming home today." I said, "I'll call you when I'm ready." I waited and waited, and about 8 p.m. that night, they cut me loose.

I got home, took a shower, and got into my own bed. Man, did that feel so good. I slept like a king. As my strength came back, I didn't realize I went from 220 pounds to 195 pounds in under a month. I had never been sick like that. But why me, God? Why did

He spare me from death? That night, I got into the shower and prayed. I prayed this to Him: "Father God, the God of Abraham, Isaac, and Jacob. The God of all creation, the God that always was and always will be, the God that sent my Lord and Savior Jesus Christ to die for my sins. Thank You for allowing me to see another day. Another day of Your mercy and grace, another day of You holding back Your wrath upon me. Father God, forgive me for all my sins I committed against You today. Forgive me for my conversations, and for sinning in my mind and in my heart. Forgive me for everything that I've done today that's unholy and displeasing to You. Thank You for being my teacher, my healer, my provider. Thank You for being my place of peace. Thank You for being my protection from the evil one. Thank You for my friends and family. I pray for each and every one of them. I pray that You forgive them for their sins they committed against You today. I pray that each and every one of our names are written in Your Lamb's Book of Life. Thank You for hearing all prayers, and thank You for answering prayers. I pray for another peaceful night of sleep tonight, and if it be Your will, that I see another day. I pray for another opportunity to please You. Amen." I have prayed that same prayer every night for the past eight years, among other things in between. I've learned not to take life for granted. What is my purpose for living? What does

God want from me? Everything I've done wrong, He still blessed me with so much. And I know I don't deserve any of it. I truly deserve to spend all eternity in hell; thank goodness for His mercy, grace, and forgiveness. I must be conscious all the time, be careful how I treat people, and know that God knows all and sees all. I've heard people say, "We are all God's children," and that is not correct. We are all God's creation, not all His children. According to John 8:44-45, it says, "For you are the children of your father, the devil, and you love to do the evil things he does. He was a murderer from the beginning and a hater of truth—there is not an iota of truth in him. When he lies, it is perfectly normal, for he is the father of liars. And so, when I tell the truth, you just naturally don't believe it!" Iota means an extremely small amount. It's an everyday fight with the evil one. He wants our souls, and it seems he is winning. This is something serious; the devil is very formidable. He convinced angels in heaven to turn against God.

Let's think about this: in heaven, where the angels have seen God and should know better, and know what God can do, they decided to rock with Satan anyway and got the beat down. Jesus said in Luke 10:18, "I saw Satan fall like a flash of lightning from heaven." My point is, our souls are on the line, and the devil wants it more than a hog needs slop. And if you listen to most of these preachers today on TV or in person, everyone who has died is in heaven. Or this saying: "Happy heavenly birthday," when, in fact, the Bible says in Isaiah 5:14, "Therefore hell has enlarged herself and opened her mouth beyond measure; and their glory, and their multitude, and their pomp, and he that rejoices, shall descend into it." In fact, Luke 13:23-28 says, "There is a great cost for anyone to enter through the doorway into God's kingdom. I tell you, many will want to enter but won't be able to." Matthew 7:13-14 says, "For the gate is narrow and the way is hard that leads to life, and those who find it are few." These few scriptures are hard to read; they scare me to death. People have said after someone has died, "I know so and so is looking down, watching over me." That's far from the truth. The truth is, according to Ecclesiastes 9:5, it says, "For the living know that they shall die; but the dead know nothing, and they no longer have a reward [here], for the memory of them is forgotten." So, whoever has died is not looking down on anything. They don't even know they are dead. I can't honestly say right now that if I died right now, I am going to heaven. I must learn the truth; what must Baron do to enter Your kingdom? A lot of people are going to hell, and I do not want to be one of them. God is opening my eyes to His word in the Bible, that's not being taught at all. The mega-churches have done a terrible job teaching the word of God. Now I'm looking for the truth. I'm keeping a watchful eye these days. The minister said, "When you see men fall, don't laugh. Learn! Learn! Because you are on your way up, and the things that tempt people to fall, you and me, are not free from that temptation, nor from the weakness that will cause us to stumble and fall. When you laugh at somebody else's fault, white or black, rich or poor, your enemy or your friend, you are laughing and opening a way for your own demise. When you do that, to laugh and not learn, to make a mockery and not to understand, is to make the same mistake yourself." So, I'm focused, remembering to learn what I can, as long as it is the truth. To learn from other people's mistakes and not do what the world does. You can't tell me anything without supporting scriptures to back it up. 2 Timothy 2:14 says, "Tell your people about these things again, in the name of the Lord, tell them not to argue over words that are not important. It helps no one, and it hurts the faith of those who are listening." 15 "Do your best to know that God is pleased with you. Be as a workman who has nothing to be ashamed of. Teach the words of truth in the right way." Romans 15:4 says, "For whatever things were written aforetime were written for our learning, that we through patience and comfort of the scriptures might have hope." Well, what Bible are the mega churches and pastors teaching from? Are they picking out all the blessings and not the punishments from God? It's all in the same book, and from

God Himself. 2nd Timothy 3:16-17 says, "All Scripture is given by the inspiration of God, and is profitable for doctrine, for reproof, for correction, for instruction in righteousness: That the man of God may be perfect, thoroughly furnished unto all good works." I've had ups and downs in my life. I have a great wife and have what I need to survive because of Him. He blessed me with a six-figure position at Costco, and blessings are still to come. More importantly, I must stay alert and be mindful in all I do to please Him. It's not easy; people can be difficult, and family can be very difficult. I had to make a decision that had me stressed out for a while. Costco is growing so fast; my location has outgrown the building. We've stretched out the hours from 6 a.m. to 2:30 p.m. to 4 a.m. until 4 p.m., just to keep up with the workload, and it's still not enough. The company has been looking for a bigger property to build a larger depot in Palm Beach County for a few years, but was unsuccessful. The property they found and purchased for the new depot is 48 miles north of the old location and 55 miles north from my house, in Port St. Lucie. I'm going from 8.6 miles from work to 55 miles there and 55 miles back, 5 days a week. That is a lot of driving, wear and tear on my car, and if I had to guess, $300 a month in gas. In my position, I'm on call once every 5 to 6 weeks, from Monday to Monday. When I'm on call, I could get a call at midnight, and I would have to get up and drive to the depot to take care of whatever the call is for. Drive back home, and get a call again at 2 a.m., turn around, and drive back again — and that's not happening. After talking to Quovadis and praying, we decided to sell our townhouse and move closer to the new location. This would be better for me, and my wife is very supportive.

CHAPTER 11

It took a little bit of time to convince her with all the pros and cons. We hired an awesome realtor; she is the bomb, a pit bull for us, and the ball is rolling. I pray it's the right decision and that God is with us. I really want to draw closer to Him so He can continue to protect and bless my household. Again, as I continue to grow older and hopefully wiser in life, I want to make better decisions, especially spiritually, because the world doesn't make it easy. I wish life could have been a little easier for everyone. It can really beat you down, and I'm so glad and blessed to have a good woman by my side through it all. A woman who knows and wants to be there with her man through the good and bad, through the ups and downs. She's stood right there with me, very respectful, and carries herself like a lady. She doesn't use profanity; she's very professional and has a big heart. She loves God, she loves me, she loves our kids and grandkids. She really works hard to be the wife God wants her to be. There have been times when I was mad at her, and she never got upset or acted unbecoming of a lady. She would still love me despite my attitude. The woman would still cook dinner, fix my plate, and bring it to me. Iron my clothes for work and turn back the bed sheets before I got in bed.

Here I am, trying to be mad, and here she is being a loving wife. It was almost like, the madder I got, the more loving she became. I used to think, "This woman must be crazy," bringing me my plate of food, trying to butter me up, being all sweet, giving me my space when I'm in my feelings. She is genuine with her love. I mean, don't get it wrong, she's not a doormat by any means; she will check you if you take her there. But she will do it with class and dignity. We both have been married to other people before, but this one is different. I've learned things with Quovadis in the past twenty-four years and am still learning each day. We enjoy each other's company; we travel all the time. In short, we have fun. We know we're not going to be here forever.

At some point, one of us is going to die first, and I pray to God, it's at a ripe old age for both of us—not sickly, just lay down for bed one night and wake up in heaven. I have some emotional things I keep inside. I don't share them with anyone, and I don't know why. One of them is my relationship with my family. My mom seems to want me to be the ever-loving son, and the Lord knows I really try to be. Why don't I go see her like an ever-loving son would or see her more often like I should? I'm doing my best to make sure she's well taken care of. The deep pain inside of me brings out my anger, thinking back on many occasions of her not being the ever-loving mother to me — making sure that I was well taken care of. She didn't. Think about when the other kids in the neighborhood got bikes and skates for Christmas, especially as I went through adolescence. I didn't get any of those things, watching the other kids ride their brand-new bikes around, and here I am walking, wishing I had a bike. Keeping me in the dark or no running water because she either went to the dog track, Palm Beach Jai Alai, the bingo hall, or played cards and lost all her money.

Moving all over the place, knowing I'm in school trying to get my education — she didn't even give it a second thought. When I saw most of the other kids' moms and dads doing what's best for the children, making sacrifices and putting their entertainment on hold to make sure the child has what's needed. Moving in and out with different people because she didn't pay the rent, even when the rent was only three dollars a month. Who in the world couldn't pay three dollars a month for rent in a brand-new apartment? I'll tell you who. My mom. She could have, but didn't. I suffered for it. Thinking about it sucks. Even now, as a grown man, it still hurts because it should not be that way. She had many doors opened for her; she had many opportunities to make better decisions. She knew plenty of well-established people she worked for, cleaning their homes and condos, and could have asked for guidance. She made me think it was okay to sit in the dark with a candle on the dresser or have no water. Dropping out of school in the ninth grade. Not coming to my field trips or high school football games. I think back and see movies, people, and hear people talk about the good times they had in college. Living in dorms, meeting new people, and just the whole experience—I didn't stand a chance to experience that. It makes me mad, sad, and wonder what my life would be like if I had that under my belt. To do your very best as a parent to provide and teach your kids, to prepare them for the world, especially since the world isn't so nice. I don't think she didn't love me, but not more than my brother or enough to prepare me for what was needed. I just wasn't important enough to her.

Now that I'm an adult, I don't have it in me to go all out for her. I made sure that my kids would never see an upbringing like that. I find myself talking to myself about it all the time. No one knows how I feel except God. She thinks I'm rich and stingy with money, and that's not the case at all. I don't let people take advantage of me. Sitting around, doing nothing, waiting for me to bring you money just because—I work and work hard for the money I make to pay the bills. Don't get me wrong, I still love her; she's the mom God gave me. Some people only want money from you, but when you try to give them advice, they don't want that at all. I'm doing okay despite all the wrong things I've done in my life, things that aren't honorable. And I ask myself, why me? Why does God bless me so much, after all the things He knows I've done, all the way down to my darkest secrets? Where did I get the drive to want to work at such an early age? Don't get me wrong, I'm glad and very appreciative of all His blessings.

I want to honor my parents, even if they're not honorable. I want to do what is right in His sight. In all my ways, I'm working to do what's right in His sight. It's not easy by any means, and yet, I am blessed. I went on a seven-day cruise. We cruised the Caribbean Sea, visiting five different islands. Great food, great entertainment, and good R&R for a few days. When I got back to work after my vacation, I was called to the manager's office. "Oh Lord, what's wrong now?" I thought, or what did I do? My manager said, "Our President of Depots and her team had a meeting while you were on vacation. They voted to give managers, based on years of service as a manager, a raise effective immediately." My raise put me in the six-figure bracket. It was a nice increase in pay for me and for all of us. What a blessing. I didn't see that coming at all. I called my wife right after and said, "Baby, we just got a raise." We both were happy as we could be. I was on cloud nine like the Temptations. The other managers knew but couldn't say anything. Where do I go from here? My walk with God must get better. I want to be a better husband, a better father, a better son, and a better employee. This is my goal in life now. I have done some stupid things over the years — a thief, a liar, a cheat, and a flat-out damn good sinner. I want to encourage people as best as I can in such a hateful world. My tests and trials I've managed by the grace of God. I don't know what the future holds for me, but I do know this: I will die one day. I will have to stand before God Almighty and explain myself.

There's nothing He doesn't already know the answer to. I will continue to recognize and learn from my failures in all that I do. Recognize the devil when he is setting me up with enticing thoughts or behavior that goes against God's law. I will push myself more to read the Holy Bible, gain understanding, and apply it to my life without wavering. It will not be easy; every day is a test. Every day is another chance to get it right. God is asking us to be obedient to Him all the days of our lives, and in turn, He will bless us all the days of our lives and welcome us into His kingdom on that day for all eternity. Never to die again. Never to suffer again. Never to be tempted by the devil again, but to live in heaven. No sadness or fear, where believers will live in a state of sinlessness and be made perfect.

But we have our part to do to get this reward. Pay attention to the deception. Don't fall asleep at the wheel, getting caught up in your emotions, as most preachers today get people into. A whole lot of babbling and not opening the Holy Bible and teaching from the Holy Scriptures. Line upon line, precept upon precept, is how it should be taught. Teach people to repent, live for the one true God, and this is my goal.

I have visions of people suffering in hell all the time. That will be for all eternity as well, where people will be tormented and punished for their sins. Where there is no hope of release. In a furnace of conscious torment where the fire never goes out. A place of misery, a place of excruciating misery where the worm does not die. Torment! This was my wake-up call. I try not to sin, but the devil has his agents dispatched. And they come at you with all guns blazing, tempting me all the time. Some days I lose, and some days I win. God knows my struggles, and He's with me all day, coaching me along the way. I must know His word to be able to defend myself against the evil one. James 4:7 says, "Submit yourselves therefore to God. Resist the devil, and he will flee from you." I don't think that means he'll flee forever. For sure, he'll be back — maybe the same day or the next. If I make it into heaven, then and only then I'll never have to worry about the evil one again. Until then, I must be ready.

God, help me, I pray. I can't do it without You. Without You, I am nothing at all. Only the truth will help me, so I dig in. I ask questions. I am mindful of the preacher whom I'm watching or listening to. All that shaking the tail feather doesn't work for me. I heard one minister say, "Schools make students, but it takes God to make a preacher." Little things like that were eye-opening to me and made me think. Churches are popping up all over the place like drugstores. Some of them are right next door to each other.

It seems everyone is called to be a pastor, with all the cotton candy preaching, not telling the people the truth about God and His divine order for us to live. And I ask again, why me? Why has He blessed me so much? I am so undeserving of all of it. This is my story, to be continued in the years to come. I pray that He allows me to live until a ripe old age, with good health and in my right mind. Thank You, Lord, for everything.

Baron Daniels

www.ingramcontent.com/pod-product-compliance
Lightning Source LLC
Chambersburg PA
CBHW051202120626
46547CB00012B/1176